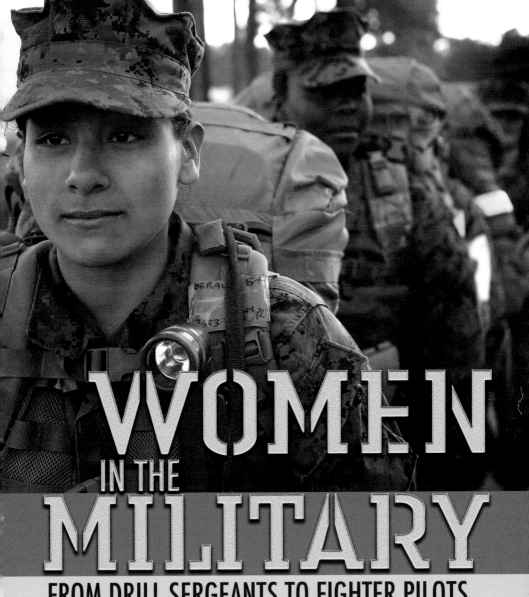

WOMEN
IN THE
MILITARY
FROM DRILL SERGEANTS TO FIGHTER PILOTS

CONNIE GOLDSMITH

TWENTY-FIRST CENTURY BOOKS / MINNEAPOLIS

*This book is dedicated to all the women
who have served in the US military.*

Twenty-First Century Books
A division of Lerner Publishing Group, Inc.
241 First Avenue North
Minneapolis, MN 55401 USA

For reading levels and more information, look up this title at www.lernerbooks.com.

Main body text set in Futura Std 9/15.
Typeface provided by Adobe Systems.

Library of Congress Cataloging-in-Publication Data

Names: Goldsmith, Connie, 1945– author.
Title: Women in the military : from drill sergeants to fighter pilots / by Connie
   Goldsmith.
Description: Minneapolis : Twenty-First Century Books, [2019] | Includes
   bibliographical references and index. | Audience: Grades 9–12. | Audience:
   Ages 13–18. |
Identifiers: LCCN 2018026893 (print) | LCCN 2018028499 (ebook) |
   ISBN 9781541557079 (eb pdf) | ISBN 9781541528123 (lb : alk. paper)
Subjects: LCSH: United States—Armed Forces—Women—Juvenile literature. |
   United States—Armed Forces—Women—Biography—Juvenile literature. |
   Women soldiers—Biography—Juvenile literature. | Women soldiers—United
   States—Social conditions—Juvenile literature. | United States—Armed Forces—
   Women—Social conditions—Juvenile literature. | Women soldiers—Crimes
   against—United States—Juvenile literature. | Sexual harassment in the military—
   United States—Juvenile literature. | Women and the military—United States—
   Juvenile literature. | Women in combat—United States—Juvenile literature.
Classification: LCC UB418.W65 (ebook) | LCC UB418.W65 G66 2019 (print) |
   DDC 355.0092/520973—dc23

LC record available at https://lccn.loc.gov/2018026893

Manufactured in the United States of America
1-44688-35527-8/22/2018

CONTENTS

CHAPTER 1
WOMEN AT WAR

I will not resign myself to the lot of women who bow their heads and become concubines [mistresses]. I wish to ride the tempest, tame the waves, kill the sharks.

—VIETNAMESE WARRIOR TRIEU THI TRINH
third century CE

One hot July afternoon in 2009, Captain Mary Jennings sat in her Pave Hawk helicopter at the American air base in Kandahar, Afghanistan. Her shift had just started and as copilot, she checked the helicopter's radios and equipment. MJ, as she was called, looked up as her crew—the pilot who led the mission, the engineer, and the gunner—jogged over to her helicopter. It was REDCON-1, time for the unit to move out.

The mission was to rescue three badly wounded American soldiers about half an hour away. The convoy had hit an improvised explosive device, a simple homemade device that detonates when a vehicle drives over it or a person steps on it. The convoy was under attack by the Taliban, the insurgent (rebel) Muslim group fighting the United States and allied troops in Afghanistan. As MJ started the rotors, three parajumpers assigned to the mission climbed aboard the helicopter with their medical supplies and gear. Parajumpers are part of the US Air Force Special Operations force and are trained for all environments. They engage the enemy in combat, if necessary, and provide medical assistance to the wounded.

MJ copiloted Pedro One Five, the lead helicopter. Its sister ship, Pedro One Six, followed behind and to one side as backup and protector. Both helicopters carried a crew of four, and Pedro One Five carried the parajumpers as well.

When Pedro One Five and One Six reached the ambushed convoy, two heavily armed US Army Kiowa helicopters were holding off the Taliban fighters so Pedro One Five could land and evacuate the wounded soldiers.

Pedro One Five's pilot executed a spectacular steep landing to avoid Taliban snipers. Two of the three parajumpers leaped out and ran toward the convoy. The third parajumper remained on board the helicopter. His role was to take over as mission leader if the pilot came under fire. The helicopter took off as soon as the parajumpers hit the ground. Pedro One Five would land again when the parajumpers radioed that the patients were stable and ready for transport. Once patients and parajumpers were aboard, the helicopters would head to Frontenac, a Canadian base not far from Kandahar.

One Five came under heavy fire soon after it took off. "I heard a crack like a baseball bat hitting a home run, and then the helo's windshield shattered right in front of my eyes," MJ wrote later in her 2017 memoir *Shoot Like a Girl*. "Through the web of splintered glass, the Kandahar desert hills stretched out for miles in front of me. . . . My right arm felt warm and wet, but I ignored it."

The crew looked at MJ in horror and shouted at her over the intercom. "For an instant all I could hear was the high whine of the engine and the deep comforting thunder of the rotor blades. I followed [the pilot's] gaze to the blood spreading over my exposed arm and the leg of my flight suit. 'I'm hit, but . . . I can still fly,'" she told her crew.

The parajumper insisted on examining her. Shrapnel had sprayed her arm and thigh. MJ's arm wound was minor, but her leg wound was bleeding heavily. The pilot radioed base to say the copilot had been hit and they were returning. Yet MJ insisted. "Look guys, I swear! I have full range of motion and my leg has already stopped bleeding. We've got three cat-A [badly injured] soldiers down there. Let's get back to it." She convinced her team to stay on task.

One of the two parajumpers on the ground radioed to say the injured soldiers were ready for pickup. He had no idea Pedro One Five had been hit by gunfire. MJ's helicopter radioed Pedro One Six for covering fire so that One Five could land. The sister ship radioed back that one of its machine guns had malfunctioned and that it could not help.

While under heavy enemy fire, Pedro One Five landed to pick up one parajumper and three patients. (The other parajumper's location was unknown.) "As the wheels touched down, heavy slugs from [enemy] machine guns began to hit us hard . . . our eight-ton [7.3 t] aircraft rocked like a little rowboat on the ocean," MJ later said. The Taliban fighters were in an excellent position—entrenched on a high hill firing down on Pedro One Five—to cause maximum damage.

Then things got *really* bad.

Pedro One Five took off carrying a very heavy load: four crew, three patients, and two parajumpers. MJ soon realized that gunfire had hit the helicopter's fuel lines. In minutes, the helicopter lost all its fuel and landed hard, while under enemy fire. Covered in blood and fuel, MJ grabbed her rifle and exited the damaged helicopter, ready to engage the enemy in active combat.

The Kiowas radioed they were returning to base to refuel and get more ammunition. The pilots said, "If you can move [fast] we'll swing by you first and take you out on the skids." The Kiowas landed. MJ and her gunner strapped themselves to the skids [part of the landing gear] of one of the Kiowas. Slowly, severely overweight and with rotors struggling to lift the load, the Kiowa took off. The pilot and engineer of Pedro One Five helped the parajumpers transfer the three patients to Pedro One Six. Then they strapped themselves to the other Kiowa's skids after the patients and paratroopers boarded Pedro One Six.

MJ saw a muzzle flash from a Taliban fighter on a nearby hill. American rules of engagement say US soldiers can only return fire if they are certain of an enemy shooter's location. This prevents hitting civilians or other American soldiers by accident. MJ remembered, "I managed to squeeze off a dozen rounds as the helo lifted off the ground. I doubted my shots could be lethal or even accurate at this range. All I could hope for was to get the enemy to duck to give us enough time to take off." It worked.

Twenty minutes later, MJ's Kiowa landed at Frontenac. She unstrapped herself from the skid. She was frantic to get to the communications hut and find out if the other members of her crew, the parajumpers, and the patients had arrived. A medic blocked MJ's way. "Captain, sir, I have to check out these wounds. I can't let you go until I take a look."

MJ remembered, "I switched my rifle to my left hand and showed him my right arm. 'See? I'm fine.'" But he insisted on looking at her thigh, covered in dried blood. Rather than waste time going to the clinic with the medic, MJ dropped her pants in the middle of the yard. "I'm not sure they noticed I was a woman under all that body armor and helmet. Now they stared openly—at my Hello Kitty panties."

Her gunner scowled at the gawking men in the yard and snapped, "What the [HECK] are YOU looking at?" The soldiers quickly turned away. The medic checked MJ's wound and said, "You're good to go . . . ma'am." Minutes later, MJ learned that everyone—crew and patients alike—had arrived safely.

CLOSE TO HEAVEN

Mary Jennings wanted to be a fighter pilot her entire life. "I knew it the first time I saw *Star Wars*. I wanted to be Han Solo, flying the *Millennium Falcon* through an asteroid field." MJ had no idea how complicated her path to combat pilot would be. In high school, she asked one of her trusted mentors to write a recommendation so she could apply for a college scholarship with the Reserve Officers' Training Corps (ROTC). This military program for college students prepares them for joining the military. But her adviser said, "Defending our nation should be left to the strong, and it's no place for a woman." It was MJ's first experience with sexual discrimination. It would not be her last.

Despite the discouraging words, MJ joined the Air Force ROTC in college and took classes to train as an air force officer. She got top grades. However, she was not selected for pilot training because she failed the physical exam due to a knee injury. Only 20 percent of air force service members become pilots. The rest choose a related specialty. MJ selected aircraft maintenance. When she reported to her first commander at her assigned post in Japan in April 2000, the major told her, "Lieutenant, the first time your time of the month gets in the way of doing your job, you're fired. Now get out of my office."

Over the next two years, MJ excelled at everything she did, from leading teams of skilled aircraft mechanics to performing complex repairs. She even used her own money to pay for civilian flight school. Yet despite excellent ratings, the air force never selected her to become a pilot. On top of that disappointment, an air force flight surgeon conducted an intrusive physical exam on MJ. The surgeon spoke to his commander about it. Minutes later, his commander called MJ to his office and asked if she wanted to press charges against the surgeon. Her own commander joined them to discuss her options. MJ decided she wanted to try to forget what had happened, and she declined to press charges against the flight surgeon. "I left the air force a few weeks later. [The doctor], as far as I know, stayed on."

MJ joined the New York Air National Guard in 2004. She hoped the National Guard would treat her with the respect her experience and abilities called for. She finally got her dearest wish. "My first time flying a jet was mind blowing. . . . Executing the acrobatic maneuvers approaching 250 miles [402 km] per hour was as close to heaven as I will likely ever get." After acing a particular difficult maneuver, she grinned at the instructor sitting next to her in the cockpit. MJ described the moment—and the instructor's comment. "That was the best spin recovery I've seen . . . from a chick."

After several years in the Air National Guard, MJ and other members of the National Guard were called to active duty in the air force. In 2007 the National Guard sent her to Afghanistan as a search and rescue helicopter pilot. During an interview in 2017, National Public Radio's *Fresh Air* host Terry Gross talked to MJ about her memoir. Gross introduced MJ this way: "In 2009, Major Mary Jennings Hegar [her married name] was shot down by the Taliban in Afghanistan while co-piloting an Air National Guard medevac helicopter. Though she was wounded in her rifle arm, Hegar managed to return fire while hanging onto a moving helicopter, which saved the lives of her crew and her patients." Because of her bravery in Afghanistan, MJ received a Purple Heart, the Distinguished Flying Cross with Valor, and several other honors. MJ left the National Guard in 2009 after her injuries. She teaches and mentors cadets (young people in military training) at the University of Texas in Austin and speaks publicly about her military experiences. In 2018 she launched her campaign to run for a seat in the US House of Representatives.

"BETTER AND STRONGER"

Until January 2016, MJ and other American women could not legally serve in combat roles. Yet women warriors have led men into combat for centuries. In 480 BCE, Queen Artemisia of Greece commanded five ships for Xerxes, the king of Persia, during a sea battle. Xerxes found her performance excelled that of his male commanders. He said, "My men have become women; and my women, men." In the first century CE, the Celtic queen Boudicca led armies against the Roman conquerors of what is modern-day England. Boudicca's armies destroyed three Roman cities in England and killed eighty thousand Romans. And in the third century CE in Vietnam, Trieu Thi Trinh rode a war elephant into battle while wearing golden armor and brandishing swords. She led one thousand warriors against the Chinese, who occupied part of Vietnam. By the time she was twenty-one years old, she had defeated the Chinese in thirty battles. Trieu is a national hero in Vietnam, with a holiday named for her to honor her bravery.

Until the twenty-first century, American women could legally fill only about nine out of ten military jobs. Combat positions were closed to them. In 2012 MJ and three other women—all of whom had served in either Iraq or Afghanistan—

sued the US Department of Defense to challenge the ban on women in US military combat positions. The case never went to court because after a three-year study, US military leaders agreed to open all positions to women if they met the same standards as men. US Secretary of Defense Ashton Carter said at a press conference in December 2015, "Fully integrating women into all military positions will make the US armed forces better and stronger but there will be problems to fix and challenges to overcome." Yet American women such as Mary Jennings, Deborah Sampson, and Sarah Rosetta Wakeman have been in combat roles. They have served unofficially and even by deception for nearly 250 years.

DEBORAH SAMPSON AND THE REVOLUTIONARY WAR (1775–1783)

Deborah Sampson was about 5 feet 8 inches tall (1.7 m), very tall for a woman of her time and taller than many men. Sampson was looking for adventure. In 1782, when she was twenty-two, she sewed a man's suit of clothes and enlisted

DEBORAH SAMPSON.
Published by H. Mann. 1797.

in the Continental Army under the name Robert Shurtleff. She joined the elite Light Infantry Company of the 4th Massachusetts Regiment. As historian Don Higginbotham wrote, Sampson used, "artful concealment of her sex," to keep her gender a secret. "Her fellow soldiers simply thought young Robert Shurtleff to be a young whiskerless lad in his late teens."

For her first duty, Sampson went to New York to scout the buildup of British soldiers in Manhattan.

Deborah Sampson disguised herself as a man to fight with the Continental Army in the Revolutionary War in the late eighteenth century. She served under the name Robert Shurtleff.

FIRSTS: SERGEANT HESTER'S SILVER STAR

In 2005 twenty-three-year-old Sergeant Leigh Ann Hester (*below*) became the first US woman to earn a Silver Star for engaging in direct combat with the enemy. This was ten years before the US military officially allowed women to serve in ground combat units. Hester, a member of the Kentucky Army National Guard, had been deployed to Iraq to protect American truck convoys. "Basically, we would go out in our Humvees and we would clear the route [of improvised explosive devices] or insurgents before the convoys would start coming through," Hester said.

Hester was a military police officer, not a member of a unit where close combat happens frequently. Yet in March 2005, insurgents ambushed the thirty-truck supply convoy that she and her unit were protecting. It was up to Hester and the other members of her unit to protect the American drivers. As rocket-propelled grenades and heavy gunfire rained down on the convoy, Hester and her squad leader ran toward three attackers hiding in a trench. At the end of a forty-five-minute firefight, Hester had killed three insurgents. In all, her unit had killed or wounded more than thirty insurgents. Only one American was injured. Hester's citation reads, "She then cleared two trenches with her squad leader . . . and eliminated three [insurgents] with her M4 rifle. Her actions saved the lives of numerous convoy members."

During the war, she fought in several battles and was wounded twice. She suffered a sword cut to the head and two musket balls to her thigh. She begged her comrades to let her die rather than risk being discovered as a woman and sent home. Instead, they loaded her onto a horse and took her to a hospital. She allowed the doctor to treat her head wound but hid her leg injury. Sampson dug one musket ball out of her thigh with her own penknife and sewed up the wound herself. She couldn't remove the second one because it was too deep to reach. The painful injury never healed properly and likely caused her pain the rest of her short life.

A year and a half into her service, Sampson fell unconscious with a fever. This time, the doctor discovered the soldier was a woman. General George Washington, leader of the Continental Army, ordered her to be honorably discharged in 1783. With the help of her friend Paul Revere, she received a military pension from the State of Massachusetts.

SARAH ROSETTA WAKEMAN AND THE CIVIL WAR (1861–1865)

By spring 1862, the Civil War between the Union (the North) and the Confederate States of America (the South) had raged for a year. It didn't look as if it would end anytime soon. Nineteen-year-old Sarah Rosetta Wakeman of Bainbridge, New York, had worked as a coal handler on a small canal boat, where she passed as a man. When Union army recruiters offered to enlist the boat workers, Rosetta, as she was called, agreed. The higher pay would help support her parents and eight siblings.

Wakeman joined the 153rd New York Volunteer Army. Women were not allowed to join either the Union or the Confederate armies, so Wakeman signed up as twenty-one-year-old Lyons Wakeman. "I knew that I could help you more to leave home than to stay there with you," she wrote to her parents. The Union army paid Private Wakeman $152 to enlist, more money than a year's wages for most young men of the time. During her time in the army, she sent much of her salary to her parents to help with the family's expenses.

Rosetta Wakeman was among the nearly 3 million soldiers who fought in the Civil War. About 620,000 died. As fatalities mounted, military officials

scrambled to fill the holes in their ranks. It was easy enough for a woman to pass as a man in those days. About 500,000 soldiers were under the age of sixteen. So a young woman who cut her hair, bound her breasts, and wore a loose-fitting uniform could easily pass as a boy too young for facial hair. Many women raised on farms were likely to be stronger than most adolescent boys and nearly as strong as men. And according to historian DeAnne Blanton, physical exams were rare, even nonexistent then. Physicians would "just have recruits walk by. And if they weren't lame or blind and if their trigger fingers worked, they were in."

So from October 1862 to February 1863, Wakeman helped defend Washington, DC, from Confederate attack. She guarded prisoners at the Old Capitol Prison there. At the prison, Wakeman learned she was not the only woman fighting as a man in the Civil War. "Over [at the] prison they have got three women that is Confined in their Rooms. One of them was a Major in the Union army. . . . When the Rebels bullets was a'coming like a hail storm she rode her horse and gave orders to the men." The Union army had jailed that woman for impersonating a man.

While with the Union army, Wakeman caught measles, then a common and often deadly infection. She was admitted to a military hospital, where she concealed her biological sex. She returned to the army after her recovery. She wrote to her father saying, "There has died out of our Regiment about 30 as near as I can learn and there is quite a number sick. We have got the measles."

The Union army sent Wakeman to Louisiana in February 1864. There she fought in the brutal Red River battles against the Confederates from March to May 1864. One of her letters home said that her regiment, "stood calmly at [its]

Women at War

post amid a shower of shot and shell, pouring volley after volley of leaden ball into the enemy, and repulsing six desperate charges."

Like many other soldiers, Wakeman also came down with chronic dysentery (a severe form of diarrhea). Diseases killed far more soldiers on both sides than did combat injuries. Wakeman was hospitalized again and was not discovered to be a woman. However, she did not recover and died in June 1864 at the age of twenty-two. Wakeman was buried in the Monument Cemetery (now known as Chalmette National Cemetery) near New Orleans, Louisiana. The name Lyons Wakeman is on her headstone.

Wakeman's family kept her secret for more than one hundred years. They also kept her letters hidden in an attic trunk. In 1991 Ruth Goodier, Wakeman's great-great niece, contacted author Lauren Cook Burgess. She told Burgess that her "great-grandmother's older sister was a soldier in the Civil War. I have in my possession copies of her letters home and a copy of her photograph." Burgess worked with family members to reconstruct Wakeman's history from her letters and edited a book, *An Uncommon Soldier*. The 1994 book contains Wakeman's letters. Her letters are the most extensive of any female soldier in the Civil War. Sarah Rosetta Wakeman was one of at least four hundred women known to have served as men in the Civil War.

CHAPTER 2
ONE HUNDRED YEARS OF SERVICE

Women who stepped up [in World War II] were measured as citizens of the nation, not as women . . . this was a people's war and everyone was in it.

—OVETA CULP HOBBY,
first director of the Women's Auxiliary Army Corps, circa 1943

Until early in the twentieth century, the only women allowed to join the American military were nurses. The US Army established the Army Nurse Corps in 1901, and the US Navy established its Nurse Corps in 1908. The United States entered World War I (1914–1918) in 1917, and for the first time, the US military allowed women who were not nurses to enlist. Tens of thousands of women served in both World War I and World War II (1939–1945). In both wars, the United States fought with its allies—France, Britain, Russia, and other nations—against Germany. During World War II, the United States and its allies also fought against Japan. During both wars, women filled military clerical and administrative roles, freeing men for combat duty.

During those years, women served faithfully and proved their value in whatever jobs the military assigned them. The military gradually became more welcoming toward women after World War II. Even so, it took nearly one hundred years, from 1917 until 2016, for the military to open up all positions—including combat roles—to qualified women.

FIRSTS: A WOMAN JOINS THE MILITARY

On March 19, 1917, the US Navy Department was preparing for the United States to enter World War I. Not enough men were enlisting, so the navy authorized women to sign up for the naval reserve as yeomen. The navy became the first branch of the military to allow women other than nurses to enlist for military jobs. Secretary of the Navy Josephus Daniels defended the decision, "It does not say anywhere [in military regulations] that a yeoman must be a man."

The first woman naval recruit in the United States was Loretta Walsh. She was sworn in on March 21, 1917, as a chief yeoman in the US Navy. Officials hoped having a woman in the navy would encourage more men to enlist. Her duties were clerical.

Twenty-year-old Loretta Walsh of Pennsylvania immediately volunteered for a four-year stint in the naval reserve. Wearing a man's uniform that she had altered to fit, Walsh was sworn in on March 21, 1917, becoming the first enlisted woman in the US military. Days later, many other women flocked to join. Rare for the time, yeomen—and yeomanettes, as some people called the women—received the same benefits and salary ($28.75 per month) as men. By the time World War I ended in November 1918, Walsh was among 11,275 yeomanettes who had joined the navy. The navy released all of them over the next year. Walsh continued on inactive reserve until 1921, the end of her four-year enlistment, although she had no military duties. She died in 1925. In March 2017, the US Navy celebrated the one hundredth anniversary of Walsh's historic enlistment with a ceremony held at the Women in Military Service for America Memorial in Arlington, Virginia.

WORLD WAR I: CLERKS AND OPERATORS

In 1917 the US Navy was the first branch of the US military to admit women to serve in roles other than nursing. Shortly afterward, the US Marine Corps (then part of the navy) did too. About thirty-three thousand American women served until the war ended in 1918. The women held the rank of yeoman. Service members with this ranking typically work as secretaries, clerks, and typists. During World War I, women operated telephone and telegraph exchanges. Some advanced to positions in military intelligence, collecting information about the enemy to assist American commanders in making decisions about how to proceed. While the army did not open its ranks to women until World War II, it hired female telephone operators to work in France as part of its Signal Corps. The operators, who were required to speak French, translated for US military staff so they could communicate with non-English-speaking Allied partners. When World War I ended, the navy and marine corps discharged their female yeomen.

The American suffragist movement—the struggle for women's right to vote—had started in the mid-nineteenth century. Among other things, women's organizations also claimed the right to equal education, to own property, and to serve their country in the military. Many women hoped that female army

units would offer them the opportunity to bear arms in defense of their nation. The Nineteenth Amendment to the US Constitution, ratified in 1920, gave women the right to vote. It did not grant them the right to serve in the military.

In her position with the US Army, Anita Phipps (*pictured in 1923*) was a strong supporter of women's participation in the US military.

One Hundred Years of Service

After World War I ended, polls showed most Americans believed women shouldn't be in the military. In 1920 Secretary of War Newton D. Baker appointed Anita Phipps, daughter of an army family, to a newly created position as director of Women's Relations, US Army. Phipps's job was to show the nation that the US Army was a progressive institution. For a decade, she advocated for a permanent place for women in the armed forces. She prepared a proposal that projected the military would need up to 170,000 military women if war broke out again. Yet Phipps had no real power, and the army rejected her plan. In 1931 General Douglas MacArthur eliminated her position. Nothing had changed. It seemed American women had no place in the military during peacetime.

WORLD WAR II: "MY BEST SOLDIERS"

When World War II started in 1939 in Europe, American women still faced enormous gender bias in the military. In May 1941, US Representative Edith Nourse Rogers (R-MA) introduced a bill to establish a women's army corps. A male representative protested, asking, Who would do the cooking, washing, and mending if women left their homes to join the military? First Lady Eleanor Roosevelt, a strong advocate for women's rights, urged that women be allowed to serve in all branches of the military. She encouraged women to join and defended those who wished to do more than type and file.

The Japanese bombed the US naval base at Pearl Harbor in Hawaii on December 7, 1941. The next day, Congress declared war on Japan and the United States entered World War II. The US military needed to dramatically increase the number of pilots, soldiers, sailors, and other military personnel. One solution was three newly created branches of the military—the WACs, WASPs, and WAVES. By the war's end in 1945, about four hundred thousand American women had served in these branches.

The Women's Army Corps (WAC). This branch of the US military was first set up in May 1942 as the Women's Auxiliary Army Corps. The corps was to be an extra branch of the US Army, and WACs did not have full military status. They received a lower salary than men did, and they did not receive overseas pay even though some worked overseas. Women in the corps received no veterans'

Oveta Culp Hobby was the first director of the US Army Women's Auxiliary Army Corps, better known as the WACs.

benefits after discharge. The initial group of eight hundred WACs entered basic training in Iowa. On the first day, they were fitted with uniforms, assigned to their companies and barracks, and vaccinated against a range of diseases. In July 1943, the WACs officially became part of the army and received similar pay and benefits as men. The army trained WACs as switchboard operators, mechanics, postal clerks, drivers, code breakers, weather forecasters, radio operators, parachute riggers, and other noncombat positions.

About 150,000 women served as WACs during World War II. General Douglas MacArthur, commander of US Army forces in the Pacific, called WACs, "my best soldiers," adding that, "they worked harder, complained less, and were better disciplined than men." Many generals wanted more women on their staffs, but public outcry made it impossible. For example, opponents of women in the military warned that Americans would view WACs as lesbians or sex workers. The army eventually disbanded the WACs in 1978, integrating women into male units, where they held many of the same jobs as men.

The Women Airforce Service Pilots (WASP). This branch, created in 1942, helped to provide Britain with more pilots. The island nation was under constant air attack by the Germans and could not train new pilots quickly enough. Jacqueline Cochran, a prominent racing pilot in the United States, convinced US lieutenant general Henry Harley "Hap" Arnold to send twenty-five civilian American women pilots to England. They would work with the British female pilots already flying in Europe. Their work would also demonstrate the skill of female pilots to American leaders. Arnold agreed. In England the American women flew planes in noncombat roles, such as moving empty planes from airfield to airfield and transporting supplies. The female American pilots were so successful that the US Army Air Forces decided to give women pilots a chance to fly planes within the United States too.

The military trained male pilots from scratch. But women were accepted as WASPs only if they had completed civilian flight training and logged five hundred hours of flight time. Civilian flight school cost about $500, which was a lot of money then. About eleven hundred women qualified to become WASPs.

During World War II, American WASPs flew military planes to US bases and assisted male pilots in target practice during training.

They clocked more than 60 million miles (97 million km) piloting military planes from the US factories where they were made to military bases in the United States. During training practice, women pilots also towed targets in the sky behind their planes for the male pilots to shoot with live ammunition.

The women's flying records equaled or excelled that of male pilots. When Lieutenant General Arnold addressed the last class of WASP cadets in 1944, he said, "Frankly, I didn't know in 1941 whether a slip of a young girl could fight the controls of a B-17 [a large plane]. . . . It is on the record that women can fly as well as men."

The WASPs never became full members of the military, and their careers abruptly ended in December 1944. The military told the WASPs they were no longer needed because enough men had returned from combat to take over their jobs. During the war, it had been acceptable for women to fly to release men for duty. But it was not acceptable to replace men once the war was over. In 1979 the military finally accepted WASPs as active duty service members. The World War II WASPs who were still living received veterans' benefits and honorable discharges for their service during the war.

Women Accepted for Voluntary Emergency Service (WAVES). This branch, established in 1942, authorized the US Navy to accept women into the naval reserves as enlistees (people who sign up for military duty and fill lower ranks). They also could serve as officers (leaders with more education and training). The WAVES could serve for the duration of the war plus six months afterward. Like the WACs and WASPs, the main purpose of the WAVES was to release men for active duty. Unlike the WACs and WASPs, the WAVES were an official part of the navy from the beginning. Women held the same ranks and received the same pay as men.

At first, governmental and naval organizations disagreed about having women in the navy. Senators, military leaders, and President Franklin Roosevelt argued over the pros and cons of allowing women to serve. By March 1942, with the United States fully committed to the war, it became clear that the navy would soon admit women. Navy officials turned to prominent female educators for guidance. Mildred H. McAfee, president of Wellesley College (a private women's

One Hundred Years of Service

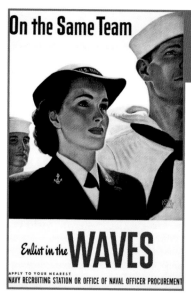

On the Same Team

Enlist in the **WAVES**

APPLY TO YOUR NEAREST
NAVY RECRUITING STATION OR OFFICE OF NAVAL OFFICER PROCUREMENT

This recruitment poster from World War II invited women to enlist in the WAVES. As part of the US Navy, they worked at many jobs, as far-ranging as physicians and engineers to coders on early computers and as aircraft mechanics.

school in Massachusetts), came up with the WAVES name. The temporary force would be all volunteers. In July, Roosevelt signed a new law that established the women's branch of the navy reserve. McAfee became the first director of the WAVES. She was eventually promoted to captain.

WAVES could not serve on combat ships or planes and, at first, were restricted to duty in the United States. Later in World War II, they served in US possessions, including Puerto Rico and in Hawaii and Alaska (then neither was a state). WAVES officers— all with at least two years of college—served as physicians, attorneys, and engineers. WAVES coders worked on early computers. Enlisted women with special training worked as parachute riggers, aviation machinists, and radio operators. The majority worked in secretarial and clerical positions.

By the end of the war, about eighty thousand enlisted WAVES and eight thousand female officers had served in the navy. By fall 1946, the navy had discharged nearly every woman from the WAVES with high praise. Secretary of the Navy James Forrestal congratulated the WAVES, saying, "You have every right to be proud. Your conduct, discharge of military responsibilities, and skillful work are in the highest tradition of the naval service."

SEGREGATION IN THE MILITARY

When Gladys Carter, a WAC during World War II, met with other female African American WACs at a reunion in 1992, they talked about segregation. "At that period of time [1942], segregation was the policy in [the United States].

Whatever segregated patterns there were in society, that existed in the Army," Carter said. "The white men, the white women, black men and black women all had separate barracks and clubs, but the uniform was the same."

While African American women led black female units, they did not escape segregation. For example, the first WAC black female officer candidates attended classes and meals with white officer candidates. But post facilities such as service clubs, theaters, and beauty shops remained segregated.

Fewer black women served in the WAVES. Training was integrated, and black WAVES were allowed to join some but not all specialty units. Living quarters often were integrated because the military felt there were not enough black women for segregated barracks. Nearly all the WASPs were white. The only black woman to apply—Mildred Hemmons Carter—was denied admission because of her race. A few Asian American and Latinas were accepted. Carter received a letter saying, "The U.S. government does not have plans at this time to include colored female pilots in the WASP." Carter later applied for Tuskegee Airmen—a group of male African American military pilots who fought in World War II. This time, the government denied Carter admission because of her

Black WACs and white WACs served in separate units during World War II. These WACs sort unaddressed and poorly addressed mail to American soldiers.

gender. (She was later accepted.) In February 2011, she received a letter from the military, recognizing her retroactively as a WASP.

During World War II, thousands of black women served in Europe and the Pacific. After the war, in 1948, President Harry S. Truman signed Executive Order 9981, officially ending segregation in the US military. Even so, the WACs—where most African American women served—did not become fully integrated until the Korean War (1950–1953). Racial integration did not stop racial discrimination in either the military or civilian worlds. Discrimination is still pervasive.

CAPTAIN KIYO SATO

In December 1941, Kiyo Sato was eighteen and in college in Sacramento, California. On December 7, the Japanese bombed Pearl Harbor, and the United States declared war on Japan the next day. On February 19, 1942, Roosevelt signed Executive Order 9066. It called for relocating about 120,000 Americans of Japanese ancestry from their homes on the West Coast to remote internment camps. The US government, with no hard evidence, feared that many Japanese in the United States were spies. Some people—including one of Sato's brothers—had enlisted immediately after Pearl Harbor and were already serving overseas in the US military. But anti-Japanese feelings were very strong in the United States. So Sato, seven of her siblings, and her parents were sent to a Japanese internment camp in Poston, Arizona, in May 1942.

Sato and several other former college students were released from Poston about five months later, in October 1942. American religious organizations, including Quakers, had arranged for them to go back to college. The rest of Sato's family left Poston in spring 1944, when her father volunteered to pick beets in Colorado. Sato completed her college degree and in 1948 received her master's in nursing from Western Reserve University in Ohio. She returned to Sacramento and worked as a public health nurse, caring for patients in the community. "It was such a surprise to be accepted in my own country to work among people who had put me away as a possible spy," she said.

Sato wanted very much to serve in the military. "After the internment, I wanted to prove I was a good American, a good citizen." She tried to join the

US Air Force nurse Kiyo Sato joined the Nisei Veterans of Foreign Wars (VFW) Post 8985 in Sacramento after leaving Korea. Nisei are American citizens whose parents were born in Japan. The VFW would not accept them as members, so Nisei vets formed their own posts.

US Army, which turned her down. So in January 1951, she joined the US Air Force Nurse Corps as a first lieutenant. She worked briefly in Texas at Sheppard Air Force Base before being transferred to Clark Air Base in the Philippines. When an officer offered her the opportunity to work in Japan, Sato accepted. She had never been to Japan and looked forward to learning about her parents' homeland. The United States was at war again, fighting on the side of South Korea in the Korean War (1951–1953). One of Sato's brothers was serving with the US military in South Korea, and she would be able to see him while she was in Asia.

In Japan, Sato cared for American soldiers who had been injured in Korea and evacuated to the hospital at Tachikawa Air Base (in Japan). The soldiers had gunshot wounds, broken bones, and concussions. "What surprised me was that many of our patients were military dependents—the wives and children of American soldiers. We had a lot of pediatric and maternity patients, and I enjoyed the work. This was a very good period of my life."

One of Sato's best memories was accompanying the flight nurses who flew with patients as they were being transferred from the Korean battlefields to the Tachikawa hospital. "As a nurse we had no military training or drilling. When I went out with my brother George and saluted someone, he told me 'You sure got a sloppy salute.' One day he took me aside and taught me how to properly salute."

Her colleagues wanted her to stay, but she had other plans. When her two-year enlistment was up, she left the Air Force Nurse Corps as a captain.

She caught a ride home on the warship USS *The Sullivans* from Japan to San Francisco. "The two years that I served in the Air Force were among the happiest in my life."

SLOW PROGRESS

Top male commanders praised the work women had done in the military in World War II. The US Congress passed the Women's Armed Services Integration Act of 1948. It authorized women to serve in the army, navy (including the marines), and air force, both in active duty and the reserves. Their roles, however, were restricted and narrowly defined. For example, women couldn't make up more than 2 percent of the armed forces. Only a few were allowed to obtain officer status. None could command men. None could serve in ground combat units or on ships—except as nurses.

By 1950 most branches of the armed forces accepted women. But enlistment declined among women as more jobs opened in the private sector. To encourage women to enlist, Congress broadened roles for women in the military in the 1960s. Lawmakers also struck down limits on the pay and rank military women could earn. Yet the US Congress stated that women were not cut out to meet the demands of combat. Full equality for men and women was not yet possible in the military.

Until the early 1970s, the United States had a mandatory draft for men. At the age of eighteen, all men were required to sign up for the military. But US participation in the Vietnam War (1957–1975) was highly controversial. Protests swept across the United States, and many young men burned their draft cards, refusing to serve. In 1973, as the war was ending, the United States decided to shift to an all-volunteer military. Increasingly, women volunteered to join. In 1993 the military dropped most restrictions for women. Women flew helicopters and jets, they commanded men, and they served on ships. Women deployed to Iraq and Afghanistan in the early twenty-first century flew on combat aircraft and helicopters. By 2006 women made up 15 percent of the US military. Yet they were still officially barred from participating in direct ground combat.

AMERICAN WOMEN IN VIETNAM

Most American men who served in the Vietnam War were drafted. About eleven thousand military women served there, all as volunteers. Of those, 90 percent were nurses. And 10 percent were air traffic controllers, intelligence officers, communications specialists, weather monitors, and clerks. The military did not yet allow women in combat, but at least eight women died in war-related incidents. Five nurses received the Purple Heart decoration for being wounded in action when the officers' quarters in Saigon was bombed.

In 1993 the Vietnam Women's Memorial—part of the Vietnam Veterans Memorial—was dedicated at the National Mall in Washington, DC, before twenty-five thousand people. The memorial is a reminder of the importance of the American military women who served in that war. About five million people visit the Vietnam Veterans Memorial each year.

The Vietnam Women's Memorial draws millions of visitors each year. Most American women who served in the Vietnam War did so as nurses, and the memorial shows a nurse tending to a wounded soldier.

Many of the beliefs that people held about women in combat have proven to be flawed. For example, the most common argument against women in military combat roles is that women aren't strong enough. In 2004 Mackubin Thomas Owens, a veteran and professor at the Naval War College in Newport, Rhode Island, wrote, "Women may be able to drive five-ton [4.5 t] trucks, but need a man's help if they must change the tires."

Army veteran and senior military instructor Master Sergeant James Gibson at Purdue University in West Lafayette, Indiana, wrote an article for a military newsletter in 2015. In it he debunked three excuses for why women shouldn't serve in combat. He said, "I have heard all the excuses on why it shouldn't happen and have seen zero concrete scientific data that shows that females cannot serve in combat arms." These excuses just don't cut it, he says.

1. *Women are not physically capable of carrying a wounded man.* "A gender neutral physical fitness test is going to alleviate that problem." A tall man weighing 220 pounds (100 kg) can carry much more than a short, 140-pound (64 kg) man. A good leader will structure his team to allow for differing physical abilities, including those of a 120-pound (54 kg) woman.
2. *The men will be more interested in the women than in doing their job.* "Every deployment I have been on, sex is against General order #1." Leaders must monitor their soldiers and discipline those who break the rules.
3. *If a woman gets injured in combat, men will focus on helping her rather than fighting.* "Male or female, it is human nature and not chivalry that makes one want to help a fellow soldier that has been wounded."

In December 2015, Secretary of Defense Ashton Carter announced that as of January 2016, women were eligible to fill all roles in the US military. This includes combat-related roles from which they have been historically excluded. The decision came after a three-year study by senior civilian and military leaders

As of January 2016, American women can serve in all military positions for which they qualify, including combat. These soldiers take a break during a training exercise.

across the US Army, Navy, Air Force, and Marine Corps. In 2012 President Barack Obama and his administration set a deadline to integrate women into all combat jobs by January 2016 or ask for specific exemptions.

The US Marines had asked for a partial exemption for machine gunners, infantry, and several other positions. Carter denied that request. He said that women will be able to contribute to the Department of Defense mission with no barriers in their way. "They'll be able to drive tanks, fire mortars and lead infantry soldiers into combat," Carter said. "They'll be able to serve as Army Rangers and Green Berets, Navy SEALs [Sea, Air, and Land Teams], Marine Corps infantry, Air Force parajumpers, and everything else that was previously open only to men."

Yet, even with Carter's decree, women faced substantial prejudice as they joined formerly all-male units. For example, in 2014 the US Special Operations Command, which oversees groups such as the Rangers and SEALs, surveyed its male members. The survey found that 85 percent opposed allowing women into their units. "It's a slap in the face telling us that chicks can do our job," one unnamed ranger said. Another ranger said, "Show me how they [women] improve the Regiment. It has been a failure integrating females in other units before. I know they can't do the real world mission."

The 2014 study found that with more training, some women can become as strong as an average man. And boot camp teaches and prepares women for all the mental and physical challenges they will encounter. Physical strength is less important in wartime than it once was. Computers, drones, and other advanced military technologies require analytical thinking rather than brute force. So the Department of Defense believes it makes no sense to generalize skills based on gender alone. Sheer brawn is no longer a requirement for combat.

CHAPTER 3
A LOOK AT THE MILITARY

I believe everyone—women and men alike—should serve a minimum tour in the military. It's an amazing opportunity. Military service builds respect, character, and independence. And you learn to honor your country.

—JENNIFER SMITHSON,
US Army veteran, 2017

The US military opened combat roles to women in 2016. Reaction to the historic change is still mixed. For example, former marine captain Greg Jacob said he found that when women entered his unit, everyone's training scores went up. "The men didn't want to get beat by the women, so they started lifting more weights, pushing harder. The entire standard of the unit was raised."

But an anonymous thirty-five-year-old marine sergeant said, "Many of the men in combat roles think of themselves as 'alpha males' and may never give 100 percent of their loyalty and trust to a female leader, even if they are told to."

In the twenty-first century, about 215,000 women serve in the US military. They make up about 15 percent of active duty service members. Other nations are way ahead of the United States. Many countries have allowed women to serve in all military positions, including combat, for years. Canada, France, the United Kingdom, and Germany allow women in combat. Poland allows women to enter every military job. It even requires college-educated nurses to serve.

Women around the world, from western Europe to Asia, have served in combat troops for many years. This woman is part of the Romanian army and is marching during a military parade to mark a national holiday.

Israeli women have been allowed in combat since the 1990s and make up about one-third of the country's military personnel. Danish women in the military perform as well as men, according to Danish research. And the Netherlands found that their military benefits greatly from mixed-gender teams, especially in crisis-response missions and peacekeeping activities.

WHY JOIN THE MILITARY?

It has been only about one hundred years since women could officially join the US military. Many civilian careers were not widely available to women in the past. Women couldn't be police officers or firefighters. Few women ran for public office or held management positions in which they supervised men. But the long struggle for women's equality has changed things for American women. They can fill just about any position for which they qualify, ranging from architect to zookeeper.

Why do women want to join the military? The military offers opportunities for growth and experiences not available in the civilian world. The military provides generous benefits, such as travel, college tuition, and health care.

THE WOMEN'S ARMY IN SYRIA

The Kurds are a minority ethnic group who live in parts of Turkey, Iran, Iraq, and Syria. The Kurds are culturally and historically related to Persians, although they speak their own distinctive language. The Women's Protection Unit (the YPJ in Kurdish) is an all-female brigade of the larger YPG, the Kurdistan armed forces, or People's Protection Unit. The YPJ makes up 40 percent of the YPG and includes Kurds, Arabs, Assyrians, and foreign volunteers. The YPG controls much of the northern part of Syria.

Kimberley Taylor (*far right*) from the United Kingdom is a member of a Kurdish YPJ unit. She sits with other members of her team in northern Syria.

The YPJ and YPG were instrumental in retaking the cities of Raqqa and Mosul in Syria from the Islamic State in Iraq and Syria (ISIS) in 2017. The YPJ and YPG's goal is to eliminate ISIS fighters. The YPJ—the women's army—also wishes to expand women's rights in the Middle East.

The women of the YPJ live together in battlefield conditions. They wear military fatigues, carry rifles, and shoot with deadly accuracy. In the 2017 documentary film *Fear Us Women*, Canadian YPJ fighter Hanna Bohman said, "ISIS believes that if they are killed by a woman, they won't go to heaven. That's an insult to them, to be killed by a woman. I wrote this poem [tattooed on her arm]. 'Fear us women, oh enemies of humanity, for you who die by our hands will burn in hell forever.'"

A Look at the Military

Women fill many different roles in the US military. These US Army service members are mechanics.

It provides a salary, housing, and food. Often the military trains people for jobs and pays them while they learn. The military also offers people intangible benefits, such as doing work with pride, gaining skills, building commitment and trust, and enjoying the camaraderie of a diverse and successful team. And many people want the opportunity to serve their country.

Jennifer Smithson was a US Army truck and helicopter mechanic for eight years. "Being in the military is an amazing opportunity, for example the chance to travel, that people may never get otherwise," she said. "Just like the civilian world there are ups and downs, tough decisions, and tough work environments. But the sense of family among your brothers and sisters in arms is even stronger than that of your own blood in many cases." The mechanical skills Smithson learned in the army served her well when she managed a Harley-Davidson dealership after discharge.

Angela Lowe is with the US Air Force. She trains military working dogs to detect explosives. She joined on a whim. "My best friend and I were watching the military channel one day after school," she said. "We looked at each other and decided it would be cool to join the air force. The next day we went to visit

Dharma Klock served in the US Army for four years. She liked many aspects of her military career but cautions women to think carefully before joining. She says the hypermasculine culture is not for everyone.

a recruiter. I was just seventeen and my mom had to sign for me to go. I saw a picture of a dog handler on a brochure and knew that was the job I wanted, even though I had never owned a dog."

Dharma Klock enlisted in the army to get out of a life she no longer cared for. "I joined when I was twenty years old, following a divorce from a man that I married too young," Klock said. "I was bored with my life, working at a dead-end job in a small Oregon town and living in my car. I was so over it! The army said you could choose where you wanted to go. I wanted to travel and leave everything else behind. So I joined with a contract that said I would go to Korea."

Shanna Reis joined the army so the military would pay her college expenses. "I was seventeen, and still in high school. My mom had to sign papers so I could join. I started boot camp a week after graduating high school and became an MP—a military police officer. I stayed for twelve years." Airman Erica Oliver works in a military hospital in Texas. She joined the air force because she was a single mother and wanted a more stable life for herself and her child.

IS THE MILITARY RIGHT FOR ME?

Many experienced military women have positive things to say about their military career. For example, Vicky Zorbas Poenitzsch, a graduate of the US Military Academy in West Point, New York, and an army captain, believes the military is a great career for men and women. "It offers unique challenges and opportunities that you cannot find anywhere else," she said. "The military has recently taken major steps to be more inclusive."

A Look at the Military

FIRSTS: SIMONE ASKEW

In July 2017, twenty-year-old cadet Simone Askew was the first African American woman in West Point's 215-year history to become a first captain—the highest position in the cadet chain of command. She will lead forty-four hundred cadets at the prestigious military college. Askew will set the class agenda, oversee the cadets, represent them at public events, and be a link between the cadets and the military administration. She said she was "humbled by the eye-opening opportunity." Askew is considering a career in military intelligence.

West Point cadet Simone Askew made history in 2017 as the first black woman to lead the Long Gray Line at the US Military Academy. She will be responsible for the overall performance of about forty-four hundred cadets at West Point.

Askew excelled in high school—in academics, athletics, and community service. She worked summers in orphanages in the Dominican Republic, a Caribbean island nation. While at West Point, she has received scholastic and leadership honors. She earned the highest female score in her class during combat field training. "Simone truly exemplifies our values of duty, honor, country," Brigadier General Steven W. Gilland, commandant of cadets, said. "Her selection is a direct result of her hard work, dedication and commitment to the Corps over the last three years."

Klock, who served four years in the army, wants young women to know that a military career can be a good option. But it's not for the faint of heart. "Young women who are unprepared to manage the sexism and hypermasculine culture will be preyed upon. It's an aggressive career choice, but I feel it's a personal choice." She says, "Sexism and harassment is a daily experience for females. It is present at all times. It shows up in blatant ways, like a male saying, 'Women shouldn't be in the military,' or in indirect ways, such as a woman not being asked to lead a squad." Smithson adds, "Today's generation is tough. I believe everyone should serve a minimum tour in the military. It builds respect, character, and independence of standing on your own two feet as well as honor for your country."

Karen Teague, a lieutenant commander in the US Navy, said, "The military is an excellent choice for girls if they are looking to broaden their horizons, are willing to better themselves beyond their wildest imaginations, and to do something few of their peers will ever get to do in their lifetimes. Often we as professional women are scared of the unknown or of trying something new. But being a military officer has taught me to not be afraid, and has enlightened me to a larger world than I ever imagined."

ARMY, AIR FORCE, NAVY, OR MARINE CORPS?

Most of the women in the US military serve in the army, followed by the air force and the navy. The marine corps, which is the smallest branch of the military, has the fewest female members. Potential military enlistees can become active duty service members, or they can join one of the reserves, which includes National Guard and reserves for each branch. Some women join the same military branch that family members did. Others seek their own unique experiences. To decide whether to join the military, people can talk to trusted mentors, research each branch, and visit military recruiters. The military often holds open houses and job fairs on bases. Military personnel also visit high schools and colleges to talk to students about job opportunities.

JOINING UP

More than 180,000 Americans enlist in the military each year and another 20,000 become officers. Only about one-fourth of young Americans who wish to enlist in the military are eligible to serve. Many people don't have the proper qualifications. They might not have the necessary education. They may have a history of illegal drug use, a criminal record, or mental or physical challenges, such as depression or obesity.

Enlisted personnel are the backbone of the military. Those who join must

- be an American citizen or hold a green card (a permit allowing foreign nationals to live and work permanently in the United States) and speak fluent English

- be at least seventeen years old (with parental consent); eighteen-year-olds do not need parental consent

- be in good health and pass a medical exam to prove it

- have a high school diploma or a General Education Diploma (GED). The diploma is necessary in some branches but not in others.

- pass a written test that includes sections on math and reading comprehension

Officers plan missions, give orders, and assign soldiers to their duties. Officers must have a college degree. There are several ways to become an officer.

- The Reserve Officers' Training Corps (ROTC) is a college program in which students take military courses in addition to the courses required for their degree. The ROTC gives members money toward their college expenses. They become military officers when they graduate. About 60 percent of new army officers come from ROTC programs.

- Individuals in professional fields such as engineering, medicine, and law can be directly commissioned as officers. The military would then send them to Officer Candidate Training Schools, where college graduates with no military experience study to become officers.

- College-age students can attend a military service academy. These include the U.S. Military Academy (Army) at West Point, New York: the U.S. Naval Academy (Navy and Marines) at Annapolis, Maryland; and the U.S. Air Force Academy near Colorado Springs, Colorado. Once admitted, students receive a four-year scholarship and other benefits such as books and clothing. They become officers upon graduation.

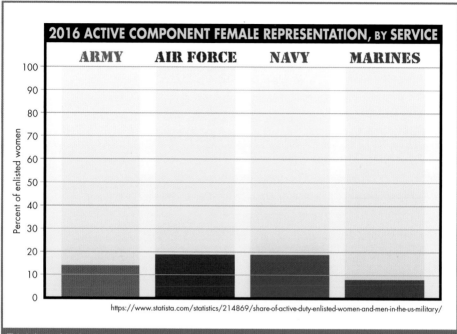

This infographic charts the percentage of female recruits in the US military, by branch. The US Marines has the lowest percentage of women while the US Navy and the US Air Force have the highest.

US Army. Enlisted women make up 14 percent of the army. The army was established in 1775 during the American Revolutionary War. The army has both ground forces and air units. Most of the soldiers in the army have a ground forces job, such as infantry (foot soldiers). The army is the largest branch of the military. Along with active duty soldiers, the army includes the army reserves (managed by the federal government) and the Army National Guard (managed by the state government where it's based). Both groups can be called for active duty, if needed.

US Air Force. Enlisted women make up 19 percent of the air force. The air force is the most recently established branch of the military. It became its own branch in 1947. Before then military aviation was divided among the army, the navy, and the marines. The air force says its mission is to fly, fight, and win in air, space, and cyberspace. It also supports ground forces by providing air support during missions. The air force has two reserve units—the Air National Guard and the air force reserves.

US Navy. Enlisted women make up 19 percent of navy staffing. The navy was established in 1775 along with the army. Its primary mission is to defend the seas, although some navy units also operate on land. The navy is the main supporter of the air force. It provides carriers for transporting aircraft. Runways on naval ships allow for aircraft landings at sea. Like the army and the air force, the navy has a reserve unit.

US Marine Corps. Enlisted women make up 8 percent of the marines. The marines were first established in 1775 as a ground force of the navy. In 1798 Congress established the marines as a separate service. Their role was to seize the beaches when the navy brought them into a mission. The marines now focus on ground force operations. The marines have their own air support, but they depend on the navy for certain air and sea operations. The marines have a reserve unit, but no National Guard. The marines want to increase the percentage of female marines to 10 percent by 2019. Major Janine Garner faced verbal sexual abuse in the marines. In a 2017 interview with National Public Radio, she said she believes that increasing the number of women in the marines will be one way to combat the culture of sexism in the military.

CHAPTER 4
WELCOME TO THE MILITARY

For me, basic training was exciting. I was aware of the "mind games" and the aggression that would be projected and I expected it. I found it thrilling when a drill sergeant started screaming at us to do push-ups.

—DHARMA KLOCK,
US Army veteran, 2017

A young recruit dressed in full combat gear and brandishing a weapon kicked in the door. Her team burst into the room, scrambling to identify hidden "enemy soldiers" in the exercise. "You're dead!" Kirsten (last name withheld for privacy) yelled from a dark corner. Eighteen-year-old Kirsten is training at Fort Benning, Georgia, to become one of the US Army's first female infantry soldiers. "I want to be one of the females to prove to everybody else that just because you're a female, doesn't mean you can't do the same things as a male."

With the Department of Defense change in policy in 2016, an estimated 220,000 more military positions opened to women. For the first time in US military history, women can serve in ground combat forces, such as the infantry, and can drive trucks, Humvees, tanks, and other armored vehicles. Women can carry rifles and handguns and use machine guns and heavy artillery in battle. Women can fly helicopters and jets into combat, and they can try out for elite units such as Army Rangers, SEALs, and other special operations units. Challenges like these are not for everyone, but many women look forward to the new opportunities.

Drill instructor Staff Sergeant Jennifer Garza disciplines her marine recruits with unscheduled physical training in the sand pit outside their barracks during boot camp training at Parris Island, South Carolina. Female enlisted marines have gone through recruit training at the base since 1949. The training is physically and mentally demanding.

It's difficult to be the first in anything—difficult to tackle challenging new roles while facing intense scrutiny and pressure to succeed. Just ask Sergeant Leigh Ann Hester, the first female soldier to receive the Silver Star for direct combat action. She hopes the Department of Defense decision will move the United States closer to ending the long debate over women in the military. "There's still people out there that don't feel that women should be in the Army, period, much less in a combat or combat support role." Progress is a good thing, she said. "It's been a long time coming."

BOOT CAMP

Whether joining the military as an enlistee or officer, new recruits start with six to twelve weeks of intense basic training, usually called boot camp. Officers may have already completed some training in a military academy or in ROTC at a university. Each branch of the military has its own training programs tailored to its specialized roles. However, all branches prepare recruits physically, emotionally, and mentally. They provide service members with the basic skills required for life in the military.

Welcome to the Military

In boot camp, every aspect of a recruit's life is managed—from meals (think food in high school cafeterias) and sleep (skimpy), to personal hygiene (timed, group showers). During the first few days, recruits receive medical and dental exams, get necessary immunizations, and receive their uniforms and training gear. Barbers cut male recruits' hair into the familiar short military buzz cut. Female members of the US Navy must have short hair. In the other branches, females can keep shoulder-length hair if they put it up into a bun or short ponytail.

Training is all about improving fitness. It consists of demanding physical activities such as push-ups and pull-ups and running while carrying heavy gear. Recruits learn rifle marksmanship, bayonet use, patrolling, marching, rappelling, basic lifesaving skills, and maneuvering through obstacle courses. They practice simulated (mock) battle and learn the history and culture of their service. The people responsible for this early training are the drill sergeants.

MEET THE DRILL SERGEANT

"A drill sergeant is a mentor, a teacher," Kaitlyn Marabello said. "Our job is to take civilians and transform them into soldiers in only nine weeks. To do this we have to completely break down who they think they are, because whoever they were before basic combat training is not who they will be after they graduate." Twenty-five years old, Marabello is a new drill sergeant with the US Army. "At the beginning of basic training, we want you to hit a low or feel like you want to quit. This helps us build you back up and teaches you resiliency, which is a fundamental tool needed for a successful soldier. Trainees have a lot to learn and they only earn the title 'soldier' after completing basic combat training." The early stages of boot camp are stressful and are meant to prepare soldiers for the chaos of battle.

It's an honor to be chosen as a drill sergeant, and the army has high expectations. The army website says, "A drill sergeant is a symbol of excellence in initial entry training, an expert in all warrior tasks and battle drills, lives the Army values, exemplifies the warrior ethos [spirit], and most importantly—is the epitome [essence] of the Army as a profession." Marabello joined the army in 2010, when she was eighteen, and completed her basic training at nineteen. She worked as a supply sergeant for several years, monitoring and tracking vehicles, weapons, radios, supplies, and other equipment. "A supply sergeant is the company commander's right hand," she said. "The commander trusts you to be accountable for property, equipment, and paperwork, because you're in charge of a lot of money and property."

After six years as an active duty soldier, Marabello joined the army reserve. She graduated from the US Army Drill Sergeant Academy in South Carolina in 2017. She returns to active duty for three months when it is time to train new recruits. "Training to be a drill sergeant was like going through basic training again, but on steroids!" Marabello continued, "We had to complete all the same demands but with more responsibility and much higher academic stressors. Out of one hundred fifteen soldiers who started the program, only seventy-three graduated. I'm proud to say I am now Drill Sergeant Marabello."

Marabello wants girls and young women to know that anything they put their minds to is possible. "You don't need to fit a mold or be the perfect poster child to be successful. School was not my strong suit and I used to get in trouble a lot. I think some of my old teachers would be surprised to learn how far I've come in the military. The point is to do your best in everything, even if it's not the same way most people do. It's okay to be different. Be true to yourself and do your personal best and you will be successful in what you do."

POWER AND SEXUAL ASSAULT

Experts know that sexual harassment, assault, and rape are unhealthy expressions of power. People in power sometimes abuse their authority by taking advantage of people with less power. In the United States, most perpetrators of violent crimes and sexual assault are men. Most victims are women. This is true in the civilian world and in the military.

Drill sergeants, especially, have a great deal of power over young recruits. The recruits may be naive and feel isolated during basic training. Some drill sergeants take advantage of this vulnerability. For example, in August 2017, the US Army suspended an undisclosed number of drill sergeants at Fort Benning, Georgia, over allegations of sexual misconduct toward trainees. After one female

Welcome to the Military

trainee stated that her male drill sergeant had sexually assaulted her, other women at the camp stepped forward with similar accusations.

Mutual consent to any sexual encounter is part of a healthy relationship—but only if both parties are of age. "Not many people know this, but a drill sergeant can be accused of sexual assault even if both parties are willing," Marabello points out. "All recruits are considered minors regardless of their age because they are trainees. While some female trainees are raped or sexually assaulted, most of the time the acts are done with consent. Even so, the army charges the offending drill sergeant with assault and rape because a trainee cannot consent per Army regulations."

Marabello says that a key part of training is to raise awareness about sexual assault and to build personal confidence among recruits. "The army requires everyone to take a class that covers sexual harassment, assault, and prevention each year. This program gives victims and survivors options. And being confident is huge. For example, I may get promoted if I'm confident in my abilities and my performance. You can't take that away from me if I don't sleep with you," she says. "And if you try, I'll report you and you'll be investigated."

GENDER INTEGRATION

Kirsten, an infantry trainee, is in the third group of recruits at Fort Benning to include women. The women objected to the plan to put their living quarters on a separate floor than their male squad mates. "There's nothing [the women recruits] dislike more than to be separated," brigade commander colonel Kelly Kendrick said. The women want to "fit in and do the same as everybody else." Base leaders listened and put the women on the same floor as the men. Cameras keep constant watch on the doors and the stairs, and a woman is always at the monitoring station. Most of the young recruits come from high school where boys and girls mingle all the time. Gender mixing in the military doesn't bother them. "They don't know any different," Kendrick said. "They don't notice they're integrated."

Gender integration doesn't worry nineteen-year-old Corbin (last name withheld). He said, "As long as [females are] pulling the weight that we're doing and we can have faith that out in the field they can have our backs while we have theirs, then let them be." The women all carry the same 68 pounds (31 kg) of gear during training. "It just makes everyone have a mindset that you can't be the last one," Corbin said. "You gotta keep striving to be better than that person in front of you."

Many countries have successfully integrated their military units. For example, a Norwegian study published in 2017 looked at gender integration in that country's military. Recruits were randomly assigned to male- or female-only living quarters or to mixed-gender living quarters. "We found that living and working with women causes men to adopt more egalitarian [equality-based] attitudes," said Andreas Kotsadam, who conducted the study. "When male soldiers shared a room with a female soldier, they were more likely to select a female candidate as a troop leader, and less likely to hold negative perceptions about female soldiers' capabilities."

IN THE MARINES

Gender-based relations have been a greater issue for the marines than for other military branches. Observers think this may be because the US Marines require males and females to train separately, which can lead to lack of familiarity and distrust. Male marines from west of the Mississippi River go through boot camp in San Diego, California. If they are from east of the Mississippi River, they train at Parris Island, South Carolina. Women entering the marines train at Parris Island, regardless of where they live. Much of their training is separate from the training men receive, and Congress has long criticized the marines for this.

Marines are the only branch of the military where men and women have not trained together. In 2017 the marines for the first time considered letting women join male-only combat training in San Diego. According to an article in the *Los Angeles Times*, "Marine Corps officials are . . . suggesting that training half of their recruits on the West Coast with no females in their units could be contributing to some of the disciplinary problems they've had. Giving the male Marines greater exposure to females during training could foster better relations and greater respect over time."

Welcome to the Military

Brigadier General Austin Renforth of the marines doesn't favor fully integrating boot camp. He estimates that 70 percent of training in the marines is integrated, and he thinks that's as integrated as it should get. He believes that weak female performance in early training will give male recruits a poor opinion of their abilities. "You get one chance to make a first impression," Renforth said. "The women, it takes them a couple weeks to understand that they can do more than they think they can do. The men come in, and they're sort of presumed brave by how they were socially engineered growing up. There's a lot of tears, there's a lot of struggling [among the women]. . . . I don't necessarily want the men to see those women. It can have a reverse effect if you see them too early."

Is Renforth expressing true concern or veiled condescension and sexism? Gillian Thomas is a senior attorney with the American Civil Liberties Union, a nonprofit organization that works in courts, government, and communities to defend individual rights and liberties protected by the US Constitution. She worries about the gender separation during marine basic training. "Our feeling is that in addition to giving sub-par training to women . . . they also come into a service where the message is sent—to them and to their male peers—that they are second class citizens. If from day one that inequality exists, then real integration is not ever going to happen."

Mixed-gender training of marines after boot camp is becoming more common. For example, male and female marines receive advanced combat training together at Camp Lejeune, North Carolina. Three female infantry marines—a rifleman, machine gunner, and mortar specialist—joined their male counterparts in 2017. Men and women have separate living quarters on base, but they share tents when they are deployed. The unit has had no unexpected challenges to integrating women into it, according to the battalion commander, Lieutenant Colonel Reginald McClam. "I joined the Marine Corps to lead Marines and sailors," he said. "I didn't take an oath of office that said I was going to lead male Marines or female Marines. . . . I said I would lead Marines."

Olumide Onanuga was a corporal and worked as an engineer with the marines for five years. His experience with women in the marines was mixed. "Some of the time it was bad for the organization but most of the time, it was

Private Tatiana Maldonado of Dallas, Texas, trains with male and female marines as she learns patrolling techniques at Marine Combat Training at Camp Lejeune, North Carolina. Gender-integrated training in the US Marines is less common than in other branches of the US armed forces. But it is becoming more common in that branch.

nothing less than exceptional," he said. "As long as women can perform the duties—that was my primary concern. Knowledge. Skills. Abilities. Some of the women could perform some jobs better than some of the men. I've met women who were faster or who could lead better than my male counterparts."

SEXUAL ORIENTATION: ANOTHER LAYER OF DISCRIMINATION

Engaging in homosexual activity had been grounds for discharge from the US military ever since the Revolutionary War. Formal policies based on sexual orientation began prior to World War II. Then the military added psychiatric screening to interviews and included homosexuality as a disqualifier for service. Gay service members—if discovered—were court-martialed [faced a military trial], put into prison, and dishonorably discharged. A policy adopted in 1944 ordered that homosexuals should be committed to military hospitals and examined by psychiatrists as mentally unfit to serve.

Fannie Mae Clackum and Grace Garner were a lesbian couple who served in the air force reserves in the late 1940s and early 1950s. Once discovered to be gay, the air force dishonorably discharged them in 1952. They demanded to be court-martialed instead. Eight years later, they won their lawsuit. Their discharges were canceled, and the two women received back pay.

The gay rights movement of the 1960s and 1970s called public attention to the issue of homosexuality in the military. Years of activism, studies, and reports followed. In 1993 Gregory M. Herek, a psychologist at the University of California at Davis and an authority on gay and lesbian issues, testified before Congress. He told the House Armed Services Committee, "The research data show that there is nothing about lesbians and gay men that make them inherently unfit for military service, and there is nothing about heterosexuals that makes them inherently unable to work and live with gay people in close quarters. The assumption that heterosexuals cannot overcome their prejudices toward gay people is a mistaken one."

In February 1993, the Department of Defense began the Don't Ask, Don't Tell policy. It prohibited military personnel from harassing or discriminating against those who didn't disclose their homosexual or bisexual status. The policy also barred openly gay, lesbian, or bisexual persons from military service. Legislation to repeal Don't Ask, Don't Tell passed in 2010. The policy

Fannie Mae Clackum and Grace Garner (*far left*) were dishonorably discharged from the US Air Force Reserves in the early 1950s when it became known they were lesbians. LGBTQ+ service members have seen progress in the US armed forces over the decades. But in the twenty-first century, they still face discrimination and higher levels of sexual assault than other members.

was to remain until top leaders certified that repeal would not harm military readiness. President Barack Obama, Secretary of Defense Leon Panetta, and Chairman of the Joint Chiefs of Staff admiral Mike Mullen sent that certification to Congress in July 2011. Don't Ask, Don't Tell ended in September 2011.

Transgender people face different challenges in the US military. Openly lesbian, gay, and bisexual service members have served in all branches of the military since 2011. Yet transgender service members risked discharge unless they passed as their biological birth sex. This meant they had to conceal their gender identities during their service. In 2015 Obama and Secretary of Defense Ashton Carter accepted that transgender people could serve openly in the military. All regulations banning transgender persons from US military service were repealed in June 2016. Qualified service members could no longer be discharged or denied reenlistment because of transgender identity. At least eighteen foreign nations allow transgender troops to serve in their militaries.

In July 2017, US president Donald Trump announced—by tweet—that transgender people would no longer be allowed to serve in the US military. The announcement sparked immediate backlash from groups within the military as well as organizations outside of the military. The tweet caught the Department of Defense off guard. The top US military officer, General Joseph Dunford, said the military would continue to allow transgender people to serve openly until the president provided direction on how to implement the new ruling.

In August 2017, fifty-six generals and admirals signed this letter to the president: "This proposed ban, if implemented, would cause significant disruptions, deprive the military of mission-critical talent and compromise the integrity of transgender troops who would be forced to live a lie, as well as non-transgender peers who would be forced to choose between reporting their comrades or disobeying policy."

In spite of strong opposition, the White House announced in March 2018 that transgender personnel would no longer be allowed to serve except in exceptional circumstances. Many Democrats and the Human Rights Campaign—the nation's largest lesbian, gay, bisexual, and transgender (LGBT) civil rights organization,

Hayden Brown (*far right*) was born female but identifies as male. From Pennsylvania he has been in the armed forces for almost five years, initially identifying as a woman. In July 2017, the president of the United States tweeted that he wanted to ban all transgender people from the military. Just days after the tweet, Brown received a call from his unit telling him he must go back to presenting as a woman if he wanted to stay in the military. Brown posted a response to the president on Facebook that went viral. His message read, in part, "President Trump, Go ahead knock me down because I'll get back up! . . . my name is Hayden Jacob Brown and I am a proud transgender soldier, serving in the United States Army."

were outraged. In April 2018, top military officials blasted the decision, saying transgender troops had not caused problems in unit cohesion or performance. As of August 2018, enlisted transgender service members remain in the military, but enlistment of new members who are transgender is still banned.

SPECIAL FORCES

All military personnel perform heroic deeds as they work to protect and defend the United States. The superheroes of the Special Forces units carry out the most dangerous and secretive missions in the military. Historically, women have not been part of these teams. But a handful of women have completed training for these specialized combat units, and others are beginning the tough journey.

About sixty thousand Special Forces operatives work under the military's Special Operations Command. Special Forces missions are highly classified (secret). Those outside of the military seldom know the details. As the nature of combat changes, military experts believe more Special Forces officers and enlisted personnel will be needed to fight terrorism. Over time more women will join their ranks.

Three of the most well-known Special Forces include the army's Green Berets, Air Force Pararescue, and Navy SEALs.

Green Berets (US Army). This group specialize in subversive and secretive operations against enemy forces. They train foreign armies to defend their own countries. They carry out missions to gather intelligence on the enemy.

FIRSTS: KRISTEN GRIEST AND SHAYE HAVER

Even before US military leaders announced that women could serve in combat, the US Army took the lead in August 2015. That month two women completed the grueling Army Ranger School. Captain Kristen Griest, twenty-six, and First Lieutenant Shaye Haver, twenty-five, graduated from the elite training school at Fort Benning, Georgia, as part of the army's gender-integrated assessment program. Haver is a helicopter pilot. Griest leads a platoon of military police. Both women are West Point graduates.

Captain Kristen Griest (*above right*) and First Lieutenant Shaye Haver look on during the graduation ceremony of the US Army's Ranger School on August 21, 2015, at Fort Benning, Georgia. Griest and Haver are the first women to successfully complete the program.

Physical fitness standards vary in the military based on gender and age. But overall women trying out for combat must meet the same standards as men. Major General Scott Miller—a Ranger himself—wanted to make that very clear. Speaking at Griest and Haver's graduation ceremony, he said, "Ladies and gentlemen . . . standards are still the same . . . a 5-mile [8 km] run is still a 5-mile run. Standards do not change. A 12-mile [19 km] march is still a 12-mile march."

The Rangers' motto is "Rangers lead the way." Haver and Griest are doing just that.

Welcome to the Military

The Green Berets' main role is fighting terrorism and other threats to national security. They also participate in humanitarian missions such as disaster relief. Green Berets may work in any environment, such as deserts, jungles, mountains, and cities.

Pararescue (US Air Force). Personnel not only parachute from planes, they are also soldiers and medics who deliver medical care to injured comrades. They must excel in swimming, running, and other physical activities. Pararescue missions usually involve the recovery and medical treatment of soldiers and downed aircrews in hazardous combat zones. Training can last up to two years and requires certification in scuba diving, emergency medical care, and parachuting.

SEALs (US Navy). These operatives work in all environments. Missions include land warfare, counterterrorism, reconnaissance, and sea operations, which require advanced diving skills. Basic SEAL training lasts one year or more. Graduates go on to earn specialty certifications as combat medics, snipers, and intelligence officers. The training is extremely demanding, and only about one-fourth of SEAL candidates graduate. As of mid-2018, no woman has become a SEAL.

CHAPTER 5
WOMEN'S WORK

I was in combat roles even before I was officially allowed to be. In my platoon we put people in the spots they were best at, and I was one of the best gunners. It was a running joke in our unit that it was all right for me to be up in the gunner's nest as long as no one back in the States knew about it.

—SHANNA REIS,
US Army veteran, 2017

In the US military, more than 750 military occupational specialties are available to service members. While women can fill any position for which they qualify, many are unlikely to opt for combat. Instead, they may focus on careers such as military police, pilot, tank or truck driver, information technology, and health care, to name a few. Or they may become dog handlers, drill sergeants, public affairs officers, or even construction workers. Meet some of the women working in a few of these careers.

REINVENTING HERSELF

The E-2C Hawkeye approached the aircraft carrier USS *Dwight D. Eisenhower* in the North Arabian Sea as it returned from a mission over Afghanistan in 2010. But the Hawkeye didn't make it to the *Eisenhower's* flight deck. One engine lost oil pressure and then failed completely. The plane could not continue on one propeller. It hurtled into the sea short of its target. Karen Teague (then a junior lieutenant) said, "My aircrew and I were about to end a day of patrolling the waters around the carrier strike force. Suddenly we heard a distress call from Aircraft 601—the Hawkeye. 'Bailout, Bailout, Bailout! Aircraft 601 bailing out!' We flew immediately towards the starboard bow where Aircraft 601 had crashed into the sea as witnessed by lookouts on the Eisenhower's bridge."

Teague was copilot and mission commander of the Sikorsky Seahawk rescue helicopter. "We were first on scene, and when we arrived our eyes were fixed on the large dome of the Hawkeye followed by the tail of the aircraft sinking into the sea. We didn't see any of the four crewmen. We immediately marked Aircraft 601's location and began our search pattern." The ideal method of recovering downed crew at sea is by dropping a search and rescue swimmer into the water with a cable attached to the helicopter. Once the swimmer finds and secures the downed airman to the cable, the helicopter hoists the airman up. Teague's crew picked up two of the airmen. The squadron's backup helicopter rescued the third.

"However, the lead pilot was nowhere to be found. That day and for the next few days, we searched tirelessly for him until he was declared 'lost at sea'. He was a fellow pilot that everyone knew," Teague said. "He made a split second decision to stabilize the aircraft as it plummeted into the sea so his three crew members could bail out to safety. It was amazing to see true heroism—the unforgettable bravery of a naval officer, who gave the ultimate sacrifice for his fellow countrymen."

Like many officers, Teague began her military career by combining ROTC with her college degree. She began flight training in 2006 while at the University of California, Davis. By 2008 she had qualified to pilot Sikorsky Seahawk helicopters. Teague deployed twice to the Middle East in 2009 and in 2010 while on board the Eisenhower.

In 2011 Teague left piloting and entered a new field. "The Navy challenges you in many ways for the better," Teague said. "It's common as you progress in your career to reinvent yourself by changing positions and responsibilities. Sometimes you may be put into a job entirely different from your intended career field." Teague attended the Naval Postgraduate School in Monterey, California.

MILITARY OCCUPATIONAL SPECIALTIES

US ARMY	Over 200—administrative services, combat operations, electronic maintenance, engineering and construction, health care, intelligence and electronic communications, mechanical maintenance, media, and public and civil affairs
US NAVY	Over 100—arts and photography, aviation, business management, computers, construction, education, electronics, engineering, finance and accounting, information technology, intelligence, law enforcement, legal, medical and dental, music, news and media, special operations, transportation and logistics, and world languages
US AIR FORCE	Over 150—administration, avionics, base operation, communications, electronics, engineering, flying/navigation, information technology, intelligence, medical professional, special forces, and weapons systems
US MARINE CORPS	Over 300 in 35 career fields—aircraft maintenance, avionics, data/communications, electronics, engineering, intelligence, legal services, logistics, personnel & administration, public affairs, and transport

Source: https://www.military.com/join-armed-forces/compare-military-jobs.html

Military.com is a website that provides extensive information about the more than 750 military occupational specialties. All are open to women, and they include the jobs above.

Women's Work

She became a human resources officer. She dealt with the hiring, administration, and training of personnel. She served as command legal officer in San Diego until January 2017.

In February 2018, Teague once again reinvented herself. She began working as an operations research specialist with the US Transportation Command at Scott Air Force Base in Illinois. She reports directly to a four-star general. She's part of a team that investigates new ideas for supply ordering. "For example, we're looking into artificial intelligence to automatically order, track, ship, and pay for large amounts of supplies. Instead of having a human perform mundane and repetitive work, we can have a machine do it. This allows people to work on more mission critical tasks." Teague hopes her story will inspire young women to reach their highest potential.

WORKING WITH DOGS

Staff Sergeant Monica Rodriguez completed several six-month deployments to Afghanistan. In 2012 she began training for the job she really wanted: an air force working dog handler. Only about 10 percent of handlers—the people who live with and train the dogs—are female. Rodriguez met her first dog, Stella, at Kunsan Air Base in South Korea in 2013. Stella had been trained to detect drugs. "It's a lot of walking through dormitories," Rodriguez said. "Just like anywhere else, people are going to be people. . . . We were policing the base." Drug-detection dogs also check vehicles entering a base and search for unwelcome intruders.

About twenty-eight hundred dogs serve in the US military. They receive extensive training, often more than a year. They learn how to detect improvised explosive devices or drugs and how to guard and patrol American bases around the world. The military trains mostly German shepherds, Belgian Malinois, Czech and Dutch shepherds, and sometimes Labrador retrievers. Dogs deployed in war zones save countless lives, both civilian and military.

When Rodriguez left South Korea, Stella stayed to work with another handler. "I was only with Stella for one year, but I formed this strong bond with her and to leave her behind with someone else was very, very difficult," she said. The dogs serve eight to nine years and usually with numerous handlers.

FIRSTS: LAUNCHING A SUPER HORNET

Directing jets to land at night on a 1,000-foot-long (305 m) aircraft carrier in the turbulent waters of the Persian Gulf is not a job everyone could do. The sailors who perform that arduous work are the catapult crew. One cold February night in 2018, a thirty-five-woman team made up the first known all-female catapult crew in US military history. Surrounded by the chaotic roar of jet engines and the blazing heat of flames shooting from their exhaust pipes, the women were operating mechanized catapults to sling the jets off the edge of the USS *Theodore Roosevelt*. They snagged incoming jets with giant hooks minutes later.

Male sailors said the work would be too difficult for women. "You're going to mess it up. You're not going to be able to do it," they told twenty-year-old Brandi Hoeft.

"No, we are going to do it. We're strong. We can do this," she replied. "Even though you are a woman, you can do the exact same thing a man can do, in anything," Hoeft added. "It doesn't have to be military related. If you say you can, you will." Within weeks, female sailors had received the training and certification they needed to become a catapult crew.

Esperanza Romero, a catapult supervisor on the *Roosevelt* said, "It's something really spectacular when you see a group of females launching a Super Hornet off the flight deck. It's a stereotype that men are constantly doing all the big, heavy-duty jobs. That's not always the case. There are women going above and beyond and doing those same jobs, and doing it successfully."

In 2017 Rodriguez was stationed at Joint Base Andrews, Maryland, as a handler. During an interview with a military newsletter reporter, she said. "Large MWDs [military working dogs] can weigh up to one hundred pounds [45 kg]. Being physically fit . . . is a crucial part of our job, especially in deployed locations," she says. "We have to have the strength to get ourselves and our dogs out of harm's way. We have to be able to lift our dogs as well as wear 50-plus pounds [23 kg] of gear." Rodriguez summed up her work. "Our job consists of blood, sweat, and tears, but that's what makes us a special breed. We are very passionate about our jobs and our partners because they are not only working dogs, they are family. We literally trust them with our life."

Rodriguez had hoped to eventually adopt Stella. In June 2017, she and Stella were reunited for good. "The thing with me and Stella is she was my first dog—so she left a huge imprint on my heart," Rodriguez said. "She was there for me when I thought I was at an all-time low and, yes, she's just a dog, but the love and selflessness a dog can give you is unforgettable. You only feel this with certain dogs. It's what I felt with Stella. We'll be giving her steak and celebrating her life and selfless service to our great country."

TALKING TO THE PUBLIC

Anna Pongo joined the Nebraska Army National Guard when she was finishing college at the age of twenty-one. Pongo didn't know how she would pay for her education or what to do with her life. "A friend and I went to see a recruiter," she said. "When I found out that I could fill a job in public affairs and that the guard offered tuition assistance, I decided to join." Because of her college degree, the guard admitted her as a sergeant in 2013.

Before Pongo went to Iraq, her duties in the guard were varied. "I got to travel across the state of Nebraska, taking photos and writing stories about what the guard was doing. We traveled to other states as well, including Minnesota and Kansas, to cover training and exercises of National Guard units there. We also traveled to Grenada in the Caribbean for Tradewinds 2016, a multinational maritime security and disaster response exercise."

After Tradewinds the guard transferred Pongo to a unit that deployed to

Iraq to help fill the US Army's 1st Infantry Division. "Active duty army and army national guard have always worked together on deployments. In this case, the unit was created specifically to provide people with skills for positions [such as public affairs] that the infantry needed but couldn't fill with active duty soldiers." During Pongo's time in Iraq—November 2016 to June 2017—she served as writer and photographer for Major General Joseph Martin, commander of Union III, a forward operating base near Baghdad, Iraq. (A forward operating base is a smaller military base that supports combat operations.) "A lot of my job revolved around telling the public what we were doing to help the people of Iraq. That included Iraqis, families of deployed soldiers back home, and news organizations," she said.

As part of her job, Sergeant Anna Pongo took this portrait of Staff Sergeant Rosie Rivera *(right)*, an executive administrative noncommissioned officer, and her husband, US Army staff sergeant Alberto Rivera. He too is a noncommissioned officer. They are one of several dual-military couples deployed to Baghdad, Iraq, with the 1st Infantry Division Headquarters and Headquarters Battalion.

Pongo's photographic and writing work allowed her to travel more often than most of the soldiers deployed to Iraq. She traveled to forward operating bases in Iraq about once a week. Not only did she meet other service members and tell their stories, she also met Iraqis. "I really enjoyed meeting them," she said. "They were always so welcoming. They fed us amazing food everywhere we went. One of my favorite things was to sit in the chow hall on base and listen to all the accents and languages going on around me."

Through her work, Pongo learned about military operations against ISIS. The United States, coalition members (including the United Kingdom, Australia, and others), and Iraqi soldiers joined together to defeat ISIS. "Each week we saw the progress the Iraqi soldiers made. The big push was to drive ISIS out

Women's Work

of Mosul [a city in northern Iraq], which had been an ISIS stronghold for more than two years. Liberating Mosul was significant, both as a symbol of hope to the Iraqi citizens, and also in freeing the hundreds of thousands of people who lived there."

Pongo returned home to Nebraska in June 2017. She works full-time for the Nebraska Army National Guard Recruiting and Retention Battalion, enlisting and retaining service members. As part of the marketing team, she helps with graphic design, social media, and advertising. "I love the military, so unless something drastic changes, I plan to reenlist when my contract expires [in 2019], and would like to become an officer one day."

BUILDING BRIDGES, MENDING FENCES

Ashley Nordmeyer's title in the Navy Seabees was E-3 constructionman. The Seabees build infrastructure, such as bridges, roads, and barracks. They repair damage after natural disasters at home and around the world. The Seabees were a natural fit for Nordmeyer. She first learned about construction when a flood hit her hometown, and she and her family demolished and rebuilt a relative's home. "I love tearing stuff down and seeing something new in its place. It's a very fulfilling feeling." Nordmeyer joined the navy in 2012 when she was twenty-two years old. "It was the most exciting and terrifying thing I ever did," she said. "Then I learned I was to become a Seabee and a builder. There are a lot of women in the Seabees. It's not every day that a woman picks hard labor, so respect is already there."

After boot camp and training that combined combat and building skills, the Seabees sent Nordmeyer to the naval station in Rota, Spain. "I helped build a gazebo [small open outdoor structure], a walkway, and put up fences. My second deployment was to the naval base in Yokosuka, Japan, where we built a seawall to protect military housing and added a room to the military police station. This was my favorite deployment. The building labor was hard, but it was good to know that you put in a hard day's work. You get to explore a new country. It's really an adventure when you make the most of it," she said. Nordmeyer toured shrines and learned about Japanese culture. She also met her husband in Japan.

Builder 2nd Class Desirae Cleary, from Modesto, California, cuts wood for trusses . She is with the Naval Mobile Construction Battalion (NMCB) 1 in the Federated States of Micronesia. Among other duties, the battalion provides construction and humanitarian support for the US Pacific Command.

Nordmeyer left the navy after five years. She and her husband—also a Seabee—had two children while she was in the navy. "When you're pregnant, the military sends you to a job where the work is not strenuous. During my first pregnancy, they sent me to an emergency operations center." During Nordmeyer's second pregnancy, she worked with the Honor Guard, the unit that provides military funeral honors.

"The navy also offered child care on base, which was a huge relief. Once your baby is a year old, you get new orders and return to a battalion," she said. "When you're deployed, you've got to sign a power of attorney [legal document] that gives someone the authority to watch your children. You miss your kids while you're gone, but you're also providing a good life for them. We all make sacrifices for our family."

Nordmeyer filled an especially important role in the military—victim advocate. "The military has an excellent sexual assault prevention program. While I personally didn't experience sexual harassment, I became a victim advocate," she said. "That means you're there for the victim as much as she needs you to be—from the victim's first phone call, then to the clinic for the detailed physical examination and evidence collection required after an assault,

Women's Work

and then to the courtroom if necessary. . . . Sexual assault can happen to anyone, anywhere. You have to protect yourself and look out for others." The military pays college costs for veterans. Nordmeyer plans to study psychology and hopes to become a military counselor.

TAKING CARE OF OTHERS

Many women learn medical skills in the military. For example, Cynthia Crate, an electronics specialist with the US Navy, taught others how to perform cardiopulmonary resuscitation (CPR) instruction and safety inspections besides her technical duties. During Crate's time with the navy (1996–2016), she took college classes. She wanted to become a registered nurse. "I picked up most of my general education requirements. My nursing school accepted nearly fifty credits from my military experience and other college classes I've done."

Erica Oliver, airman first class, US Air Force, completed basic training in 2017 and then became a medical technician. She works at San Antonio Military Medical Center in Texas, considered one of the best hospitals in the nation. "I assist the nurses and doctors with patient care. We do all of the hands-on stuff like starting intravenous lines, drawing blood, and all sorts of other cool things. In the trauma room, I'm in charge of monitoring the patients' vital signs, and if needed, I perform CPR until advanced life support is administered. It's a stressful but rewarding job and I enjoy every minute of it. I plan to finish my Bachelor of Science in Nursing degree and commission as a captain upon completion."

Vicky Zorbas Poenitzsch served as a captain in the Medical Corps in the US Army from 1997 to 2002. She managed medical services at a hospital in Thailand during Operation Cobra Gold, an annual multinational military exercise. "I was an ambulance platoon leader supporting the 25th Infantry Division. I coordinated medical services for the missions in which—among other services—we treated dehydration and snakebites. We also worked in HIV/AIDS prevention training, as it was an epidemic in Thailand. I know that work helped to improve relations in the region."

FIRSTS: SECOND LIEUTENANT MARIAH KLENKE

In October 2017, twenty-four-year-old Second Lieutenant Mariah Klenke became the first female marine to graduate from the marine's Assault Amphibian Officer Course. This 29-ton (26 t) vehicle operates on land and in the water. Typically, it carries twenty-five marines and their equipment from a navy ship to an enemy beach and as far inland as necessary. It works just as an armored tank would on land.

In the fall of 2017, US Marine second lieutenant Mariah Klenke received her certificate at the graduation ceremony for completing the Assault Amphibian Officer Course at Camp Pendleton, California. She is the first female assault amphibian officer in US military history.

The twelve-week course followed Klenke's Officer Candidate School, where new officers learn the essentials of command. She had to prove herself by completing a 150-pound (68 kg) deadlift (lifting weights off the floor to hip level); a 115-pound (52 kg) clean-and-press (lifting weights off the floor to above the head); and dragging a 215-pound (98 kg) dummy to simulate rescuing a wounded soldier. A background in competitive sports helped prepare Klenke for these physical challenges.

Klenke was the only female in her group. She felt the males treated her as an equal. "We were all good friends in the class, so it was just friendly jokes about everything," she said. One of the biggest challenges was a week at Camp Pendleton, California, where the students were doing three to four missions a day. "It involved a lot of planning. . . . We were working on a couple of hours of sleep a night." Klenke is confident she chose the right field. "After a year of training, I'm finally just excited to get my platoon and start working for them, training them."

CHAPTER 6
SEXUAL HARASSMENT AND ASSAULT

Sexual assault violates the core values of our military and must never be tolerated. We have more work to do to advance dignity and respect for each and every person. Far too many of our people find their lives changed by this crime and there are far too many who continue to suffer in silence.

—REAR ADMIRAL ANN M. BURKHARDT,
US Navy, 2017

In January 2017, the US Marines accepted its first group of women trainees for a marine infantry combat unit. Less than a month later, a disturbing pattern of behavior surfaced among male marines. A private Facebook site called Marines United had transformed from a group for building friendship and emotional support among male marines to a revenge porn site. One member had posted a collection of nude photos of female service members without the women's knowledge or consent. In some cases, male marines had secretly photographed women in showers or dressing rooms and posted those photos. In other cases, women allowed intimate partners to take nude photos and videos, likely trusting they would remain private. As the photos and videos circulated, members wrote obscene comments about the women. Some of the men joked about sexually assaulting the women.

Tom Brennan, a marine veteran and editor-in-chief of the military newsletter the *War Horse*, was a member of Marines United. When Brennan realized what was happening, he was horrified and wanted to act. He began to collect screenshots and directories of the photos so he could report the

US Marine Corps veteran Erika Butner (*right*) came forward to speak about her life and career after photos of her were posted on the Marines United Facebook page. She and attorney Gloria Allred (*left*) spoke in September 2017 in Washington, DC, at a press conference about new legislation. Titled the Servicemembers Intimate Privacy Protection Act (SIPPA), the law would prohibit military service members from sharing intimate images without the consent of the individuals in the photos.

illegal activities to marine leadership. More than thirty states and the District of Columbia have laws against posting sexually explicit images and videos without the consent of the person photographed. Doing so is a crime in the US Navy and US Marines as of April 2017. Brennan met with military authorities several times in January and February 2017. The US Marines fired the man who had posted the first set of illegal images. Facebook administrators deleted the images and took down the Marines United page. Yet the photos and videos popped up on new sites. And when members of the original Facebook site discovered that Brennan had notified the military authorities, some marines threatened him and his family with violence and even death.

CYBER SEXUAL ASSAULT

The US Marines kept the story quiet until Brennan broke the story publicly. In March 2017, he wrote an article in the *War Horse*. He said, "The US Department of Defense is investigating hundreds of Marines who used social media to solicit and share hundreds—possibly thousands—of naked photographs of female service members and veterans." He went on to say that "more than two dozen women—many on active duty, including officers and enlisted service members—have been identified by their full name, rank and military duty station in photographs posted and linked to a private Facebook page." Because of Brennan's article, the Naval Criminal Investigative Service and the US Congress immediately opened investigations.

Christina Cauterucci, a staff writer for the online magazine Slate, wrote, "These disturbing revelations paint a picture of a military culture in which men are building feelings of camaraderie around the exploitation of their female peers. This is the same tactic used by boys in middle school and high school, who create secret 'slut pages' on social media, where they distribute any private nude photos they get from girls in their grade." An investigation by the Naval Criminal Investigative Service in 2018 determined that the majority of the photos were selfies or were posed for and then voluntarily shared. However, it is unlikely that the women agreed to massive public distribution of the photos.

Then Secretary of Defense Jim Mattis said the unproven actions "represent egregious [appalling] violations of the fundamental values we uphold at the Department of Defense." General Robert B. Neller declined to comment on the specifics of the case. However, the marine commandant did tell CNN that "for anyone to target one of our Marines, online or otherwise, in an inappropriate manner, is distasteful and shows an absence of respect." The corps' highest-ranking noncommissioned officer (unnamed) challenged marines to look in the mirror and decide if they are part of the problem or the solution.

In June 2017, a marine pleaded guilty to participating in the Marines United site. He was convicted by court-martial. His sentence included serving ten days in military prison, a demotion of three ranks, and a fine equaling two-thirds of his monthly salary. In the following months, officials investigated 108 more male marines for the same crime. Of the 60 who received punishment, 7 were court-martialed, 7 were kicked out of the military, and the rest received other administrative discipline.

Yet the same photos, estimated at 131,000 images, kept appearing on new sites. They were shared on hard drives, stored in the cloud, and put up for sale on the dark web. (The dark web is a secret part of the World Wide Web, accessible only with specific software, where illegal activities such as selling pornography or fake identities takes place.) The ongoing harassment and distribution of the photos sparked the term *cyber sexual assault*.

#NOTINMYMARINES

In March 2018, CBS reported that more photos—involving women from all branches of the military—had been discovered spread across numerous online social media sites. In 2017 US Marine veteran Erin Kirk Cuomo had founded

#NotInMyMarines, a group dedicated to ending sexual harassment and assault in the military. She discovered the photos and turned them over to investigators. "One year later and not much has changed," Cuomo said. She added that formal military policies for dealing with sexual assault are in place and appropriate and that a deep-rooted culture change is still needed in the military. "Step up [Department of Defense], we demand action," she urges.

THE SOLDIER

What exactly are sexual harassment and sexual assault? Sexual harassment is repeated instances of unwelcome sexual advances, requests for sexual favors, suggestive language, and obscene comments. Sexual assault is touching a person in an intimate manner without consent, and forcing sexual contact up to and including rape by coercion, drugs, or violence. Dharma Klock (army) and Cynthia Crate (navy) were not involved in the US Marines cyber sexual assault scandal. But they both faced sexual harassment and assault on a nearly daily basis in their combined service of fourteen years.

During Klock's four years in the army, she was in South Korea, Poland, the Czech Republic, Germany, Kuwait, and Iraq. As a transportation specialist, she often drove large fuel tankers and tractor/trailer combos in war zones. "We entered Iraq on the second or third day of Operation Iraqi Freedom [the first US entry into Iraq, intended to overthrow the dictator Saddam Hussein] in 2003 as support troops," Klock said. "We were frequently targeted with bombs, IEDs [improvised explosive devices], small arms fire, and ambushes."

Overall, the military was not a good experience for Klock. "I knew after the first year that I would not stay in the army after my four-year contract was up. I had idealized the military and believed it was disciplined and gave you a chance to thrive. What I found was a hypermasculine society that displayed poor discipline and integrity."

In Klock's case, the army's hypermasculine culture took the form of sexual assault. "I was saved at the last minute by another male soldier kicking in the door and grabbing me from underneath the male soldier who was pulling down my pants," she said. "Some of my female soldier friends were raped. Some reported it and some did not." According to Klock, many of the women who came forward were shunned or experienced further harassment and horrific backlash because they had "caused trouble."

"I could go on about how many times I was sexually harassed or almost assaulted. I was resilient and quickly developed a sense of what was going on. Some of the men called me by the nickname 'firecracker' for responding to harassment in an extremely aggressive way. I would cuss them out, threaten and humiliate them, anything so the men would learn I was not someone to mess with. After my near-rape experience, I grew my armpit hair out and would show it to the men and watch them cringe. I wanted them to be disgusted and to view me as someone that was not available sexually."

THE SAILOR

Cynthia Crate served ten years in the navy. The navy sent her to Africa, the Mediterranean, and to the Middle East. She went as part of Operation Enduring Freedom, the war against terror in response to the terrorist attacks on the United States on September 11, 2001. Although many male members of Crate's family had joined the military, she was the first woman. She worked in highly technical fields such as electronic warfare and anti-ship missile defense. She provided specialized training to other sailors and performed inspections.

"The military can be a very rewarding career," Crate said. "I learned that hard work paid off, and if I worked just as hard as my male counterparts, then they had more respect for me. I've seen women who tried to use their sexuality as a tool to get ahead. For example, the man I worked for on my second ship chose a female sailor for a job that should have been mine because I was more senior and had more experience. She slept with him, while I did not."

One man harassed Crate so much that she was uncomfortable at work. "I had to report him and things got even worse. The top enlisted person on the ship was a female. She told me that I wasn't a good enough First Class Petty Officer because I wasn't able to stop him myself," she said. "I went to the Executive Officer; he took it seriously and so did the Captain. They stopped the harassment, but it harmed my career. For example, I received lower evaluations in [reviews] and that leads to fewer promotions. There were other incidents, but that one was probably the most damaging."

What advice does Crate have for young women contemplating a career in the military? "It's tough being in the military as a female, but it has gotten better over the years. The military is made up of all kinds of people just like the whole country is. There are good and bad people anywhere you go. Work hard and learn the job you are training for. You can do anything you set your mind to."

WHO IS AT HIGHEST RISK?

In 2016 for the first time ever, the Department of Defense Annual Report on Sexual Assault in the Military asked active duty service members about their sexual orientation. About 5 percent in the report said they identified as lesbian, gay, bisexual, or transgender. Despite the 2011 repeal of the Don't Ask, Don't Tell rule, LGBTQ+ peoples are at higher risk for sexual harassment and assault in the military than are straight service members. ("Q+" includes people who define themselves as "queer" or "questioning" or "other." Language for transgender, queer, and other peoples differs depending on the institution, year of the study, and other factors. In this book, the language of original sources is preserved.)

More than 18 percent of military women who do not identify as LGBT have experienced sexual harassment, while about 28 percent of LGBT military women were sexually harassed. The difference in rates of sexual assault was also significant. Sexual assault among straight women was 3.5 percent, while more than 6 percent of women identifying as LGBT reported being sexual assaulted.

An article written by PhD student Sitaji Gurung at the City University of New York found that sexual orientation discrimination against LGBT remains strong. "This is a vulnerable population often ignored due to various forms of oppression," Gurung said. "We owe a lot to our brave LGBT service members who serve in the military despite this oppression."

Another group of service members who experience high rates of sexual harassment and assault are black women. The African American Policy Forum is dedicated to advancing and expanding racial justice, gender equality, and human rights. According to the group, black women make up nearly

Sexual Harassment and Assault

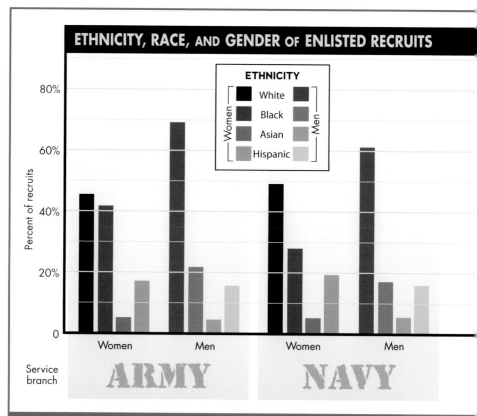

ETHNICITY, RACE, AND GENDER OF ENLISTED RECRUITS

ETHNICITY

Women
- White
- Black
- Asian
- Hispanic

Men

Percent of recruits (80%, 60%, 40%, 20%, 0)

Service branch

Women — Men — **ARMY**

Women — Men — **NAVY**

Women, particularly women of color, make up a significant percentage of service members in all branches of the US military. They and their LGBTQ+ comrades are at much higher risk of sexual assault in the military than are other members of the US armed forces.

one-third of the female population of the US military. Yet they generally hold lower ranks than white females despite having more years of service. "This power imbalance causes Black women to experience sexual harassment and assault at a disproportionate rate," according to its website. About one in three black women experience sexual assault during their military service. Gurung points out the "need for strong accountability and oversight to protect . . . minority persons while they are serving their country."

REPORTING AND REPRISAL

The Rand Corporation is a prestigious nonprofit research institution that focuses on improving policies and decision-making. A 2014 Rand Corporation study

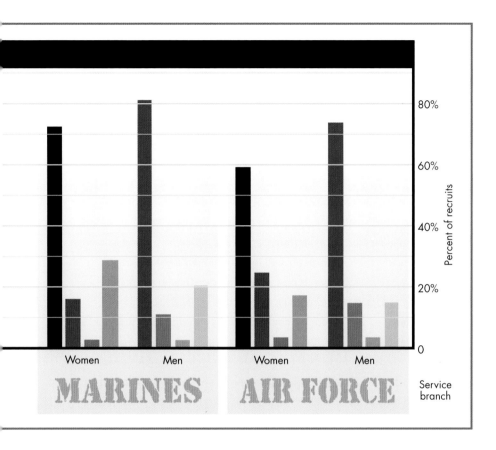

80%

60%

40%

20%

0

Percent of recruits

Women   Men   Women   Men   Service
branch

MARINES   AIR FORCE

of female active duty members found that 25 percent of women "might have experienced" sexual harassment or discrimination, while 5 percent of women "might have been" assaulted. Victims often choose not to report incidents of sexual harassment and assault. Why? Many times the victim is aware she will not be believed or will not be taken seriously. She may be ashamed and embarrassed and not want other people to know about it. She may fear that others will retaliate or find ways to take revenge. A woman may experience more harassment or assault if she reports an incident. It may damage her career and cost her a promotion. Retired US Air Force colonel Don Christensen said, "You're much more likely to be retaliated against than you are to see your attacker prosecuted."

A woman who complains of harassment or assault may receive a diagnosis of mental illness and because of that a less-than-honorable discharge. In

Sexual Harassment and Assault

2016 the nonprofit Human Rights Watch issued *Booted: Lack of Recourse for Wrongfully Discharged US Military Rape Survivors*. The scathing report documented numerous examples of reprisal after women service members reported sexual assault.

For example, Airman First Class Juliet Simmons was one of many women Human Rights Watch interviewed for *Booted*. Simmons was drugged and raped while serving in the air force. She reported her assault through the proper channels. That usually means reporting the incident to an immediate supervisor or other person in charge. Simmons continued to do her job and received excellent performance reviews. Yet she was required to see a military mental health provider and was diagnosed with a personality disorder. Though she appealed, she was discharged and unable to return to the military. "Why should I be discharged because I was raped?" Simmons asked. "I did what I was supposed to do. Had I never come forward, I truly believe I would still be in the Air Force."

Booted—which took more than two years to research—chronicles so-called bad paper discharges. These are military discharges with a less-than-honorable status. Service members with that status and a diagnosis of mental illness receive either no veterans' benefits or lesser benefits than those with an honorable discharge. And while women make up about 15 percent of the military, they receive 30 percent of bad paper discharges. Once discharged, the impact of a less-than-honorable discharge in the civilian world can be catastrophic. They may face discrimination in the workforce and have difficulty finding a job. They may also lose custody of their children if the terms of discharge are serious enough. Having this type of discharge has also been linked to higher rates of homelessness, arrest, and suicide.

In April 2018, several anonymous US officials provided early details of a report on military sexual assault by the Pentagon (the headquarters of the Department of Defense, near Washington, DC, in northern Virginia). Reports of sexual assault increased 10 percent in 2017: 8 percent in the army and more than 9 percent in the navy and air force. However, sexual assault in the marines jumped by nearly 15 percent. Experts aren't sure if the increase shows a growing problem or if more victims are coming forward.

According to a 2017 Public Broadcasting Service article, "Defense officials have argued that an increase in reported assaults is a positive trend, because it's a highly underreported crime. . . . Greater reporting . . . shows there is more confidence in the reporting system and greater comfort with the support for victims." Yet the previous year's report revealed that well over half of those who had reported their assault experienced retaliation ranging from forced night marches with heavy backpacks, to loss of a position, to a diagnosis of personality disorder and discharge without benefits. With this low rate of reporting and high rate of retaliation among those who do report, many think the Department of Defense's claim of increased trust in the system is unfounded.

In May 2017, US Naval Academy midshipman second class Sheila Craine (*far left*), a sexual assault survivor, testifies before the US House Armed Services Committee's Subcommittee on Military Personnel. She is seated with (*from left to right*) Ariana Bullard, Stephanie Gross, and Annie Kendzior. Kendzior, a former midshipman, and Gross, a former cadet, were both raped twice during their time at their military academies. A Pentagon survey found that 12.2 percent of academy women and 1.7 percent of academy men reported unwanted sexual contact during the 2015–2016 academic year. The number of such reports at West Point and at the Naval Academy has ticked upward over the last academic year.

Sexual Harassment and Assault

While Annie Kendzior was a cadet at the US Naval Academy, two male cadets raped her. She reported the assault, but the academy eventually threw her out after a review board found her medically unfit to serve. The rapists were never punished. In 2017 Kendzior testified before the US House of Representatives Armed Services Subcommittee. She told lawmakers that "[rape victims] are frequently and intentionally left behind to deal with the pain, anguish and long-term emotional stress while the rapist's career continues without any consequence."

Experts—as well as victims—believe that removing the reporting of assault from the military chain of command will result in better outcomes and more support for victims. Kendzior recommends that civilian police—not military staff—investigate rapes at military academies. She also believes an independent prosecutor should investigate cases, rather than someone in the chain of command, such as the victim's immediate supervisor.

Nichole Bowen-Crawford was in her early twenties and went to Iraq during Operation Iraqi Freedom in 2003. A fellow soldier raped her when they were working the night shift. Although Bowen-Crawford told her supervisor what happened, he said it would hurt her career if she complained. "People in the military can't report sexual assault or harassment without retaliation," she told a journalist for Public Radio International, "because they have to use their chain of command [to report an incident], and oftentimes [people in] the chain of command are the perpetrators."

In 2013 US senator Kirsten Gillibrand introduced the Military Justice Improvement Act to remove the reporting of military sexual assault from the chain of command. The US Senate voted down the bill in 2014 and 2015. In 2016 it didn't even vote on Gillibrand's bill. Late in 2017, Gillibrand again introduced the bill in the Senate. As of June 2018, the Senate website states the bill's status is "Read twice and referred to the Committee on Armed Services." The bill has an estimated 21 percent chance of being passed by that committee. Opponents of the bill say that commanders are essential to maintaining order and discipline and that removing them from the process would undermine the system. Gillibrand said that military sexual assault is as pervasive as ever.

New York senator Kirsten Gillibrand is flanked by Sarah Plummer (*left, in blue*), a US Marine Corps veteran and victim of sexual assault, and Kate Weber (*far right, in gray*), a veteran who was sexually assaulted during her service in the US Army, during a news conference in Washington, DC, in November 2013. Gillibrand proposed a law allowing military prosecutors rather than commanders to make decisions on whether to prosecute sexual assaults in the armed forces. At far left is Senator Richard Blumenthal (D-CT). Senator Dean Heller (R-NV) stands behind Gillibrand at center.

#METOO

In 2017 hundreds of thousands of women responded to the Twitter hashtag #MeToo. They publicly disclosed years of sexual harassment, abuse, and assault while working in entertainment, government, journalism, sports, and business. In just a few days, more than 1.7 million #MeToo tweets went global. Twelve million Facebook users wrote #MeToo on their timelines, and many shared their stories. In December 2017, *Time* magazine named the #MeToo movement as its Person of the Year, referring to the women behind the movement as the Silence Breakers.

A group of active duty and retired female service members held a rally at the Pentagon in January 2018. Monica Medina, assistant to Leon Panetta, former US secretary of defense, spoke: "[The Pentagon] is where I joined . . . the #MeToo club. This club is not one I wanted or even admitted being a part of until a couple of months ago," she said. "But today I am here to tell my story in public for the first time. I was sexually harassed [at the Pentagon] and it changed the course of my career. When it happened, I was young and had no one to help me do anything about it. Sexual harassment is the problem that really needs our

The US military provides mandatory sexual assault prevention training through its SHARP program. This SHARP poster promotes the military's stated position about sexual assault and harassment.

attention. . . . This is the moment. #MeToo is the movement and the military needs to use this moment in time to encourage women who are victims of harassment to come forward."

The US military has been working quietly to reduce sexual harassment. However, the public outcry has focused on the issue and increased pressure on the military to act more forcefully. "There is no room for sexual harassment in the military or anywhere for that matter," Karen Teague said. "I believe the military has become a leader in combating this type of behavior through increased training on how to deter inappropriate conduct [and how to foster a] culture of respect for one another and exemplary actions from a majority of our leaders. It's unclear if this behavior has decreased, as I do not believe we had good measurements of actual incidents. But reports and investigations are more prevalent and taken more seriously than ever before."

One way in which the army is working to reduce and ultimately eliminate sexual offenses is its Sexual Harassment/Assault Response and Prevention (SHARP) program. It provides mandatory training to enlisted personnel and officers. It plans to achieve its goal through cultural change, prevention, intervention, investigation, and accountability. The program's website says, "You are my brother, my sister, my fellow Soldier. It is my duty to stand up for you, no matter the time or place. I will take ACTION. I will do what's right. I will prevent sexual harassment and sexual assault. I will not tolerate sexually offensive behavior. I will ACT."

FIRSTS: MARINE CORPS INFANTRY OFFICER

In September 2017, the first female officer graduated from the grueling US Marine Corps infantry officer training course in Quantico, Virginia. The second lieutenant (whose name has not been publicly released) will command a forty-person platoon. Typically, one-fourth of all applicants fail the eighty-six-day course. About 10 percent drop out the first day when officers hike fourteen hours with an 80-pound (36 kg) backpack and complete an obstacle course that requires climbing a 20-foot (6.1 m) rope several times. The second lieutenant is the only woman to complete the course out of thirty-six who have tried so far.

Infantry troops are the first marines to enter a war zone. While every marine learns basic infantry skills, only about one out of five marines becomes part of the elite infantry. According to Teresa Fazio, a former captain in the marines and writer for the *New York Times*, "[The female marine corps infantry officer's] graduation . . . paves the way for women in combat arms not to be a big deal in the future. Like her male classmates, this officer has met an exceptionally high standard. Soon, she will be just one more Marine infantry lieutenant, picking up her first platoon."

The lieutenant joined her new unit, based at Camp Pendleton, California. Fazio wrote, "This female officer can be a key tactical asset to her unit if they deploy to Afghanistan. . . . Female troops are invaluable for searching houses and communicating with local women, gaining access to spaces and information that, because of local custom, male troops cannot get."

Sexual Harassment and Assault

CHAPTER 7
INVISIBLE VETERANS

When I came home from Iraq, I felt invisible as a woman vet. No one looks at me and thinks, "combat veteran."

—KAYLA WILLIAMS,
US Army veteran and director of the VA Center for Women Veterans, 2017

Jenny Pacanowski, a former combat medic in Iraq, knows how it feels to be an invisible veteran. When she attends veterans' events, she often gets what she calls the crossover handshake. She described it to a journalist. "You know the one, right? When some guy reaches right over me to shake hands with a nearby guy. 'Thank you for your service,' they say to the man next to me! Even though I'm the Iraq War veteran, I'm the one who drove a military ambulance through the Sunni Triangle [a dangerous area northwest of Baghdad, Iraq]." Pacanowski grew so frustrated at not being recognized as a veteran that she had the words "Combat Veteran" tattooed on her arm. "I shoulda got it tattooed on my forehead," she joked.

The *Washington Post* chose Veterans Day 2017 to publish an article to debunk several myths about women veterans. Perhaps the biggest myth is that there aren't very many of them. When people think about veterans, they're usually thinking about men. Yet women make up more than two million of the nation's twenty-one million veterans. The article quoted a report from Disabled American Veterans, which found a perception that

Jenny Pacanowski is a former combat medic who is also a poet, facilitator, and public speaker. She leads writing workshops for veterans throughout the United States to help ease the transition from military culture to civilian life.

"a woman who comes to [a Veterans Administration medical facility] for services is not a veteran herself, but a male veteran's wife, mother, or daughter." This can make her feel like an invisible veteran.

"TO CARE FOR HIM . . . AND FOR HIS WIDOW"

The motto of the Veterans Administration (VA) perpetuates the invisibility of female veterans, according to Allison Jaslow. She is chief of staff of the Iraq and Afghanistan Veterans of America, the largest organization representing post-9/11 veterans. "The Department of Veterans Affairs has a woman problem," she said. "Need evidence? Look no further than its motto: 'To care for him who shall have borne the battle and for his widow, and his orphan.'"

That motto dates back to April 1865 when President Abraham Lincoln gave his second inaugural address. The American Civil War was ending, and Lincoln spoke about that. "Let us strive on to finish the work we are in, to bind up the nation's wounds, to care for him who shall have borne the battle and for his widow, and his orphan, to do all which may achieve and cherish a just and lasting peace among ourselves."

Lincoln was speaking when women did not serve officially in the military. His reference to widows and orphans showed his intent for the US government to provide for the families of the soldiers who had died in battle. Nearly one hundred years later, in 1959, the VA adopted Lincoln's words as its motto. The words are inscribed on hundreds of plaques mounted on the walls of VA hospitals and clinics across the nation. But Lincoln's words eventually became obsolete as women joined the military and left behind widowers and orphans of their own.

Invisible Veterans

The Iraq and Afghanistan Veterans of America argues that the motto makes female veterans invisible. Jaslow said, "Every day that the VA preserves this motto, it ignores and obscures the needs of far too many women veterans."

Kayla Williams, director of the Center for Women Veterans (a department of the VA), said the VA is moving toward a modernized version of the outdated motto. The new motto says, "To care for those who shall have borne the battle and their families and survivors." Yet instead of completely replacing the old motto, the VA is incorporating the new one alongside the original. What purpose does retaining the original motto serve in today's military? Many female veterans see no purpose and feel that it actually perpetuates gender stereotypes.

VA MEDICAL CARE FOR WOMEN

Medical care is a benefit for veterans of the American military. The care is usually provided at VA hospitals or clinics. More than one-fourth of female veterans are enrolled in the VA health-care system. According to the Center for Women Veterans—a branch of the US Department of Veterans Affairs—about five hundred thousand female veterans receive care at 170 medical centers and 1,063 outpatient medical clinics nationwide. Even so, women often encounter barriers and obstacles. For example, when entering a VA clinic, women veterans are often mistaken for companions of male vets seeking care. Women want and deserve to be recognized as veterans themselves. And the majority of women prefer a female physician, but the VA has few on staff. Some VA facilities do not offer mammograms, gynecological examinations, and maternity care for women vets. (One-third of VA medical centers don't have a gynecologist.) Even something as basic as privacy may be hard to come by. Many examining rooms have only curtains rather than doors. Often female veterans have to use the public women's restroom. Male veterans use restrooms set aside specifically for them.

Williams has a hopeful view of services for women veterans. In a letter to the Iraq and Afghanistan Veterans of America, she reported that the VA outperforms private health-care sectors in providing gender-specific care to woman veterans. For example, breast cancer screening among women is 86 percent in the VA compared to 74 percent in the private sector. The rate for cervical cancer screening in the VA is 88 percent, compared to 76 percent in the private sector. Williams added, "VA provides prenatal and preconception care, maternity care services, and 7 days of newborn care for women veterans. . . . We recognize that there are ongoing improvements needed within VA [and] are working diligently to identify challenges and opportunities facing women veterans."

COMING HOME

During Shanna Reis's twelve-year stint with the Army National Guard, the army deployed her to Afghanistan and then to Iraq. During her first deployment in 2004, Reis was a radio operator. She was so eager to get home after her yearlong deployment that she declined the mental health services the military offers to all returning soldiers. Things were fine at the beginning, but then depression set in.

"It was kinda like a slow creep where I felt something was wrong and it just got worse and worse and worse. I became very paranoid," Reis said. "I was convinced that as soon as I closed my eyes something was going to happen. And then that kind of led to sleeplessness and I started getting audio hallucinations of events that happened. And it just [kept] building and building into more paranoia."

Reis was among the 11 percent of Afghanistan veterans who suffer from post-traumatic stress disorder (PTSD) due to traumatic events such as battles, injuries, or seeing comrades badly wounded or killed. "I kind of retreated into my room. . . . And I just stayed there in like this little cave that I made. And I did not come out. I did not interact. I stopped working. . . . And I slowly got better. But it was slow and a very nightmare-ish process for me. I did not . . . reach out for help at all. I dealt with it myself."

In 2008 the military called on Reis for a second tour of duty. She was deployed to Iraq for a nine-month stay as a military police officer. She knew she didn't want to go through the paranoia and depression she had experienced after her first deployment. So she accepted the mental health services the military offered before she went home. "They took each individual soldier and

Invisible Veterans

sat us down in front of a medical officer who said, 'There's help available. Do you think you will need it?' And I straight up said Yes. I am gonna need it." Reis encourages veterans to reach out. "That's the hardest part of it . . . the talking out loud. Not only so someone else hears it—but so that you hear it. And that was the thing that seemed to help me the most. It kind of forced me to sit there and process everything."

Mental health counseling helped Reis avoid another depressive episode. But she feels she is not getting all the benefits she is entitled to. "The VA is a maze, and getting anything out of them is like trying to roll a boulder up a hill," she says. "I have some benefits, but there are more that I should be getting that I am not. I'm too tired of dealing with the VA to fight over it anymore."

Joana Garcia retired from the navy after twenty years fixing fighter jets on aircraft carriers. She wanted to do something new: voice-over acting and specializing in audiobook recording. She decided to use her VA educational benefit to train for that work. "Unfortunately, the military denied me this training because I already had degrees in another field. Then I tried to obtain benefits through the VA's Vocational Rehabilitation Program, but that didn't work either. After months of trying to work with the program, the task became too discouraging. I decided to save the fight for another day."

The transition from military to civilian life can challenge women veterans in other ways too. Sarah Maples, an air force veteran and a director of the Veterans of Foreign Wars, wrote, "Operating in male-dominated environments and doing traditionally male activities, up to and including combat, are so different from the experiences of civilian women that the two sides often cannot relate. Moreover, the behaviors—male behaviors—that women veterans learned were correct in the military are now at odds with the expectations civilians have for women."

Transition programs to help veterans returning to civilian life are still often geared to male rather than female veterans. This is changing slowly. For example, in 2016 the US Army established a new mentoring partnership with private corporations. The goal is to help military women transition to civilian life. Program founder Sidney Goodfriend said, "The women's program will focus

Job programs for military service members help veterans transition to civilian life.

on women veterans who will get women mentors who are seasoned executives from all types of different big and small companies around the country." The program includes activities such as learning to write a résumé without using military acronyms. Women in the program also role-play through recorded interviews to improve job-hunting skills. Ultimately, most women manage the challenges of life after deployment and successfully reintegrate into civilian life.

SUICIDE

Like men, women vets may experience post-traumatic stress disorder. LGBTQ+ and straight female veterans may also suffer from military sexual trauma if they experienced repeated sexual harassment or sexual assault during military service. Because of high rates of this disorder, especially among vets returning from Iraq and Afghanistan, female and male veterans are at risk for depression and suicide. For example, up to 20 percent of Iraq veterans experience post-traumatic stress disorder. Military sexual trauma, financial stress, drug use, and social isolation among vets—either during deployment or upon returning home— also increase the risk for suicide.

Suicide rates for all American women have risen in recent years. About 40,000 people die from suicide in the United States each year and 23 percent—9,200—of them are women. The suicide rate for civilian women is 10.2 out of 100,000 women, but the suicide rate for women veterans is 17.3 out of 100,000. According to a 2016 article in *Current Psychiatry Reports*, there is little difference between suicidal thoughts and attempts by LGBT and heterosexual veterans within a year of discharge. Yet LGBT veterans are more than three times likelier to have suicidal ideation—thinking about suicide—over a lifetime, compared with straight women. The Suicide Prevention Center wrote in 2014 that while some sources suggest a higher rate of suicide among LGBT women, information on sexual identification isn't put on death certificates. More research is needed into the suicide risk for female LGBTQ+ veterans. As more female LGBTQ+ troops serve openly in the military, many people believe the additional research will begin.

"Women veterans should know that VA can help, including through counseling at vet centers, which are predominantly staffed by other veterans," Williams said. "In fact, 25 percent of vet center employees are women veterans who have served in a war zone!" Besides counseling, behavioral therapy, medication, and hospitalization, if needed, can help. Perhaps most helpful are support groups where female veterans can openly talk about their experiences. Women are more likely to open up about their post-traumatic and military sexual trauma than are men, according to Williams.

A 2018 interview on National Public Radio focused on the difficulty female veterans may experience when moving from military to civilian life. Host Jay Price said, "Meetings for female veterans have been occurring . . . all over the country with support from the VA. The idea is to build a gender-specific support

HELP FOR VETERANS

VETERANS CRISIS LINE:
1-800-273-8255

CALL 24/7, TEXT, OR CHAT ONLINE.

system." He also pointed out that "VA experts on women's mental health say the transition to the civilian world has long been a priority [for the VA]."

HOMELESSNESS AMONG WOMEN VETERANS

Dr. Shad Meshad, a psychologist and veteran of the Vietnam War, realized long ago that benefits and services needed to be tailored for specific groups of veterans. "I'm reminded of the years I spent counseling vets before PTSD was a recognized diagnosis," he said. "In those years, we had to learn how Vietnam vets were different from WWII and Korean War vets. Now we have to focus on how women veterans are different. . . . We're trying to identify women just before or just after they leave the military so we can connect them to the resources they need—therapy, jobs, housing, VA benefits, etc."

The VA estimates that between twenty thousand and forty thousand female veterans are homeless. And while 33 percent of female service members are black, they make up 45 percent of homeless women veterans, according to the African American Policy Forum. Female veterans are two to four times more likely than civilian women to be homeless.

However, unlike many homeless male veterans, most women don't sleep on the streets or in shelters. Instead, they may couch surf at the homes of relatives and friends. Or they may sleep in their cars. They may remain in unsafe, abusive relationships to keep a roof over their heads. Homeless women veterans don't show up in the same places as men do. So the VA is not always able to accurately count women vets in their studies of homelessness. BriGette McCoy, an army veteran with a history of military sexual trauma and homelessness asks, "How do you serve a population that's so well-hidden, who stays under the radar because they're traumatized?"

The VA reported in 2017 that homelessness among veterans dropped by 47 percent between 2010 and 2016. That's good news. But the figures didn't separate women and male veterans. With women consistently undercounted, it's unclear if homelessness in women veterans actually decreased. The VA doesn't recognize couch surfing as homelessness. "I guess (to the federal government), if you have a couch, then you're OK, even though it's not your couch," said

As a veteran, Sandra Strickland (*in checked suit*) was once homeless. She advocates for female vets, including testifying before Congress about their specific challenges and needs.

Jas Boothe, a sixteen-year army veteran who was once homeless. When Boothe tried to get the resources she needed to find a home, "They told me that since I had an illegitimate child, I should go to the welfare office and get food stamps."

Many young women enter the military right out of high school and have never lived alone or found their own housing or paid their utility bills. While in the military, service members don't need to think about those chores. Yet immediately after discharge, veterans become responsible for everyday tasks. Some discover they're unprepared to perform these common duties. They may live with domestic abuse, be seeking a divorce, or have few family or social support networks.

More than half of homeless female veterans are diagnosed with a mental disorder—real or perhaps documented on a bad paper discharge—or have been treated for military sexual trauma. Many areas of the United States have a shortage of affordable housing. And not all veterans are able to find jobs that pay a living wage. It's not difficult to see why some women veterans are unable to provide homes for themselves and their children. The Veterans of Foreign Wars has called on the US Congress to expand job training for vets.

FIRSTS: TAMMY DUCKWORTH

Retired US Army lieutenant colonel Tammy Duckworth has been a Democratic US senator from Illinois since 2017. She has several firsts to her credit. A former army helicopter pilot in Iraq, she lost both her legs when a rocket-propelled grenade hit the helicopter she was copiloting in 2004.

After years of public service, Duckworth became the first female double amputee to serve in the US Senate. She is the first member of Congress born in Thailand. She is the first senator to give birth while in office. After the

birth, fellow senators soon changed the rules so that female senators have the right to bring their infants onto the Senate floor and breastfeed them there. Duckworth was the first to do so in April 2018 when she cast a vote on the floor of the US Senate while holding her ten-day-old daughter Maile.

Senator Tammy Duckworth leaves the US Senate in Washington, DC, after casting a vote. She brought her newborn daughter, Maile Pearl Bowlsbey, with her as part of Take Your Daughters and Sons to Work Day on April 26, 2018. Maile became the first newborn allowed onto the Senate floor during a vote.

The group also wants to see more employment benefits for all homeless veterans to help resolve these issues.

Some women face problems while in the military and after discharge. The majority value their service and enjoy the camaraderie of other service members. Jennifer Smithson puts it this way. "When you take an oath, part of your oath is protecting each other and in some cases, making the ultimate sacrifice," she said. "You've got each other's back 24/7. It even extends to when you leave the military. No matter the time or the distance, you can always count on your brother and sisters in arms. You also have so many opportunities at your fingertips: the travel, education, joining in on community events, sports, and more." Many women go on to enrich their lives through those experiences. They may enter new careers, work to help other veterans, or even run for public office.

CHAPTER 8
SUCCESS AFTER SERVICE

The military can be an amazing experience for young women. I've seen my own personal growth: becoming confident, learning new things, and gaining experiences that would be next to impossible to get without the military.

—SERGEANT ANNA PONGO,
US Army National Guard, 2017

Kayla Williams feels the media focuses too much on the problems that female veterans face rather than on their strength, resilience, and contributions to their communities. "Compared to our male counterparts, women veterans are more likely to have college degrees and to work in management or professional occupations," she says. "We have significantly higher average household incomes than women who have never served. We return to our communities with leadership and technical skills and a high propensity to serve in new ways through volunteering and other forms of civic engagement."

MOVING ON, MOVING UP

Returning women veterans are assets to their communities in many ways. For example, Jennifer Smithson works in a senior living facility as an activities director, and she is pursuing a college degree. Dharma Klock is a social worker with a master's degree. She specializes in addiction and mental health issues. Erica Oliver, an air force medical technician, plans to work on her nursing degree, which will entitle her to become a captain. Cynthia Crate obtained many college credits while serving in the navy. After discharge, she enrolled in nursing school and has nearly completed her nursing degree. And when Vicky Zorbas Poenitzsch left the army, she went to graduate school and earned a PhD in chemistry.

Women vets bring many professional skills into the civilian world when they leave the US armed forces. Erica Oliver, for example, wants to continue to use her medical skills in civilian life.

Shanna Reis turned her love of sculpture into a bachelor of fine arts degree. The VA covered much of the cost as an educational benefit for veterans. She works in a children's museum in her hometown. "Job-wise I feel like I am still trying to find something that will stick. If my job with the museum goes well I hope to have more time to work on my art in the future."

Joana Garcia achieved her goal of becoming a professional voice-over actor who records audiobooks. She wants to help other veterans do the same. "Many veterans who fought for this country are coming home with severe physical or mental injuries," Garcia said. "I want to help those who cannot work outside of their homes to set up their own voice-over businesses. The veterans need to know they can bring joy and happiness through reading amazing stories aloud which may reach thousands of people."

Jas Boothe took helping others to a whole new level. After experiencing homelessness as a veteran, she founded the nonprofit organization Final Salute. The organization has helped at least two thousand homeless female veterans find a safe place to live. Boothe also sponsors the Ms. Veteran America contest each year. The event highlights the courage, strength, and sacrifices women make in the military. The contest has raised more than $330,000 to fund housing for women veterans and their families. Boothe has appeared on several television shows. CNN, *Redbook* and *People* magazines, the Department of Defense, the YWCA, and the American Veteran's Center have also honored her work with awards and public recognition.

LET'S TAKE A VOTE

According to a 2017 Iraq and Afghanistan Veterans of America member survey, veterans vote in elections far more often than do civilians. For example, 58 percent of registered US voters chose to vote in the 2016 presidential election, while 88 percent of veterans voted. And more than four out of ten veterans have considered running for office.

At the national level, political representation in the United States is skewed heavily toward male politicians. For example, half of the American population is female, yet only one out of five members (20 percent) of the US House of Representatives is female. Of the one hundred US senators, only twenty-one are women (21 percent). The #MeToo movement, the women's marches of 2017, and a renewal and revitalization of the women's movement have led to a surge of women seeking to fill congressional seats to right the balance. In the midterm elections in November 2018, a record number of women ran for seats in the US House of Representatives and the US Senate. As of August 2018, more than 525 women were running for office in the November 2018 midterm election. That's a 67 percent increase from 2016.

Many of them were veterans who felt their military experience gives them an edge. "I think my experience gives voters a certain sense of comfort that I can do the job," Mikie Sherrill said. Sherrill is a former navy pilot with a background as a federal prosecutor. She announced in 2017 that she would run against twelve-term Republican Rodney Frelinghuysen for a seat in the US House of Representatives in the 2018 election. Frelinghuysen announced his retirement early in 2018 when it became apparent that several candidates had a better chance of winning. Sherrill won the Democratic nomination in a landslide victory in the New Jersey primary in June 2018 to make her the Democratic candidate in the November 2018 general election.

Mary Jennings Hegar, a former air force helicopter pilot, said "I believe in

Amy McGrath was one of several female military vets running for political office at the national level in the 2018 midterm elections. A Democrat, she ran in Kentucky for a seat in the US House of Representatives.

using diplomacy first and military strength as a last resort," she said. "Practicing isolationism, alienating allies, enacting travel bans, and creating a divided nation only serve to weaken us and our place on the world stage." Hegar, who won a Distinguished Flying Cross for Heroism and a Purple Heart for her bravery in Afghanistan, ran for the US House of Representatives as a Democrat from Texas in 2018. Hegar won the nomination in a landslide victory in the Texas primary in June 2018. She ran as the Democratic candidate in the November 2018 general election against eight-term Republican John Carter.

When Amy McGrath was thirteen years old, she wrote to her Kentucky congressman to tell him about her dream of flying fighter jets. He wrote back saying that women should be protected and therefore not allowed to serve in combat. Nevertheless, she persisted. She achieved her dream and became the first woman to fly in an F/A-18 Hornet on a combat mission. After a twenty-year career as a US Marine Corps jet fighter pilot, McGrath ran in 2018 for the US House of Representatives. She won the Democratic nomination in her district in Kentucky in the May primary and became the Democratic candidate for the November 2018 general election.

Chrissy Houlahan of Pennsylvania, who served in the air force and is an engineer, ran for a seat in the US House of Representatives in 2018. "It's not necessarily the skills that one gains in the military," she said, "but the perspective as an active-duty member." Houlahan won the Democratic nomination in her district in Pennsylvania in the May primary to become the Democratic candidate in the November 2018 general election.

Gina Ortiz Jones is a former US Air Force intelligence officer. She announced in January 2018 that she wanted to run for Congress out of frustration with the policies of President Donald Trump and his administration. She won the Democratic nomination during the June 2018 primary for a seat in the US House of Representatives and went on to run in the November 2018 general election. She said that, if elected, she would be the first lesbian, first Iraq War veteran, and first Filipina American to represent Texas in Congress.

AT THE LEADING EDGE

Karen Teague strongly believes the military is an excellent choice for young women. "You may always wonder what it would have been like if you didn't join the military," she says. "But if you join, you will have great and wonderful experiences in your life, and tough, challenging moments, just like you may come across in any job in the civilian sector. The difference is you'll have been at the leading edge of your country's operations dealing with worldwide issues with your brothers and sisters in arms. Opportunities are abundant if you seek them out."

Military life poses significant challenges to women in many ways. Yet most are proud of having served their country and feel their time in the military was an important part of their lives. And as women continue to break barriers by joining every area of the military—including combat units—military culture will shift from a male-dominated organization to an institution where women are fully accepted, treated as equals, and encouraged to excel.

Navy lieutenant commander Karen J. Teague began her navy career as a pilot. Her personal decorations include two Navy and Marine Corps Commendation Medals, a Navy Achievement Medal, and other unit and service awards.

TAMMIE JO SHULTS SAVES THE DAY

The airplane engine exploded at 30,000 feet (9,144 m) while the aircraft was traveling at 500 miles (805 km) per hour from New York City to Dallas on April 17, 2018. Pilot Tammie Jo Shults radioed to air traffic controllers, speaking in a calm voice. "We have part of the aircraft missing, so we're going to need to slow down a bit. We've got injured passengers."

The controller asked if the plane was on fire and Shults said, "No, it's not on fire, but part of it's missing. They [flight attendants] said there's a hole, and uh, someone went out."

The explosion had scattered sharp-edged metal debris from the engine into the passenger cabin, shattering a window.

In April 2018, Captain Tammie Jo Shults calmly piloted Southwest Airlines Flight 1380 as it experienced engine failure between New York and Dallas. The plane landed safely, and she and crew members and passengers of the flight were invited to the White House the next month to meet with the president.

The sudden loss of air pressure in the cabin was sucking a female passenger out through the broken window. Fellow passengers pulled her back into the cabin. She later died from her injuries.

Shults calmly and successfully made an emergency landing in Philadelphia, saving the lives of 148 passengers, 7 of whom had minor injuries. People who knew her weren't surprised. After all, she'd been one of the first female fighter pilots for the US Navy. Shults knew she wanted to fly as a young girl and had attended a lecture on aviation as a senior in high school in 1979. She was the only girl there. The colonel giving the lecture saw her in the auditorium and asked her if she was lost. "I mustered up the courage to assure him that I was not and that I was interested in flying. He . . . assured me there were no professional women pilots." But Shults didn't let that stop her. When she learned the US Air Force wouldn't let her fly, she joined the navy in 1985 instead. Women could not fly in combat zones at the time. But she helped train male pilots to fly the F/A-18 Hornet fighter/attack aircraft in Operation Desert Storm (1990–1991). Shults left the navy in 1995.

She became a commercial pilot and saved the day—and lives—on that April morning in 2018. "She has nerves of steel," passenger Alfred Tumlinson said. "I'm going to send her a Christmas card . . . with a gift certificate for getting me on the ground. She was awesome."

Timeline of Historic Advances for Women in the Military

1901   The US Army establishes the Army Nurse Corps.

1908   The US Navy establishes the Navy Nurse Corps.

1917–1918   More than thirty-three thousand US women serve as nurses and in military support positions in World War I.

1942–1943   In World War II, the US military establishes the Women's Army Corps (WACs), the Women's Airforce Service Pilots (WASPs), and Women Accepted for Volunteer Emergency Service (WAVES). More than four hundred thousand women serve in the US military during World War II.

1948   Congress passes the Women's Armed Services Integration Act granting women permanent status in the military and entitling them to veterans' benefits.

1950–1953   During the Korean War, about 120,000 US women in the army, navy, and air force serve in Korea and Japan, mostly as nurses.

1965–1975   About 265,000 American women are in the military around the world. About 10,000 serve in Vietnam, mostly as nurses.

1973   The military draft for men ends in the United States. The all-voluntary military creates opportunities for women to serve in hundreds of noncombat military jobs.

1976   Females are admitted to the nation's military service academies: U.S. Military Academy (Army) at West Point in New York; Naval Academy at Annapolis, Maryland; and Air Force Academy at Colorado Springs, Colorado.

1990–1992   More than forty thousand women serve in the Persian Gulf War in noncombat roles in war zones.

1993–1994   The US military allows women to serve on most warships and to train as fighter pilots and other combat aviation jobs.

2003–2011   In the Iraq War, American female pilots fly combat missions for the first time.

2010   Female officers deploy on navy submarines for the first time and fill leadership positions.

2016   The US military opens all positions, both combat and noncombat, to women who qualify. The names, dates, and locations of deployments are not made public.

2018   The air force names its first female air commando brigadier general.

Source Notes

4 Trieu Thi Trinh, quoted in KeriLynn Engel, "Trieu Thi Trinh, the Vietnamese Joan of Arc," Amazing Women in History, March 1, 2012, http://www.amazingwomeninhistory.com/trieu-thi-trinh-the-vietnamese-joan-of -arc/.

5 Mary Jennings Hegar, *Shoot Like a Girl: One Woman's Dramatic Fight in Afghanistan and on the Home Front* (New York: Penguin, 2017), 219.

5 Hegar, 219.

5–6 Hegar, 219.

6 Hegar, 220–221.

6 Hegar, 224.

6 Hegar, 235.

7 Hegar, 238.

7 Hegar, 240.

7 Hegar, 240.

7 Hegar, 241.

7 Hegar, 241.

7 Hegar, 15.

8 Hegar, 21.

8 Hegar, 51.

8 Sarah Maples, quoted in "The Inconvenience of Being a Woman Veteran," Atlantic, November 22, 2017, https://www.theatlantic.com/politics/archive/2017/11/the-inconvenience-of-being-a-woman-veteran /545987/.

8 Hegar, *Shoot Like a Girl*, 97.

8 Hegar, 99.

9 "A Purple Heart Warrior Takes Aim at Military Inequality in 'Shoot like a Girl,'" *NPR*, *Fresh Air*, March 2, 2017, http://www.npr.org/2017/03/02/517944956/a-purple-heart-warrior-takes-aim-at-military -inequality-in-shoot-like-a-girl.

9 King Xerxes, quoted in *Herodotus, Books 7 and 8*, trans. Caroline L. Falkner, 2001, http://www.stoa .org/diotima/anthology/artemisia.shtml.

10 Ash Carter, quoted in Cheryl Pellerin, "Carter Opens All Military Occupations, Positions to Woman," Department of Defense, December 3, 2015, http://www.defense.gov/DesktopModules/ArticleCS/Print .aspx?PortalId=1&ModuleId=753&Article=632536.

10 Don Higginbotham, quoted in, "American Heroes: Deborah Sampson, Soldier of the Revolution," A Patriot's History of the United States, accessed March 21, 2018, http://www.patriotshistoryusa.com/teaching -materials/bonus-materials/american-heroes-deborah-sampson-soldier-of-the-revolution/.

11　Leigh Ann Hester, quoted in Rachel Martin, "Silver Star Recipient a Reluctant Hero," *NPR*, February 22, 2011, https://www.npr.org/2011/02/22/133847765/silver-star-recipient-a-reluctant-hero.

11　Hester, quoted in Ann Scott Tyson, "Soldier Earns Silver Star for Her Role in Defeating Ambush," *Washington Post*, June 7, 2005, http://www.washingtonpost.com/wp-dyn/content/article/2005/06/16/AR2005061601551.html.

12　Sarah Rosetta Wakeman, *An Uncommon Soldier: The Civil War Letters of Sarah Rosetta Wakeman, Alias Private Lyons Wakeman*, 153rd Regiment, New York State Volunteers, ed. Lauren Cook Burgess (Pasadena, MD: Minerva Center, 1994), 9.

13　DeAnne Blanton, quoted in Brigid Schulte, "Women Soldiers Fought, Bled and Died in the Civil War, Then Were Forgotten," *Washington Post*, April 29, 2013, https://www.washingtonpost.com/local/women-soldiers-fought-bled-and-died-in-the-civil-war-then-were-forgotten/2013/04/26/fa722dba-a1a2-11e2-82bc-511538ae90a4_story.html?utm_term=.ae9c282a5f5d.

13　Wakeman, *Uncommon Soldier*, 44.

13　Wakeman, 44.

13–14　Wakeman, 11–12.

14　Ruth Goodier, quoted in Wakeman, preface, xv.

15　Oveta Culp Hobby, quoted in Kay Bailey Hutchinson, "Women's History Month," Humanities Texas, March 2012, http://www.humanitiestexas.org/news/articles/womens-history-month-oveta-culp-hobby-senator-kay-bailey-hutchison.

16　Josephus Daniels, in Jessica Meyers, "Celebrating the First Enlisted Women," Department of Defense, March 22, 2017, https://www.defense.gov/News/Article/Article/1127379/celebrating-the-first-enlisted-women/.

19　General Douglas MacArthur, quoted in Melissa K. Wilford, "'My Best Soldiers': Thirty-Six Years on the Women's Army Corps," US Army, October 7, 2008, https://www.army.mil/article/13127/my_best_soldiers_thirty_six_years_of_the_womens_army_corps.

21　Henry Harley "Hap" Arnold, quoted in Dora Dougherty Strother, "Women of the WASP," accessed March 21, 2018, http://www.wingsacrossamerica.us/wasp/resources/dora.htm.

22　James Forrestal, quoted in "3rd Year: WAVES number 86,000," All Hands, August 1945, https://www.ibiblio.org/hyperwar/USN/ref/AH-4508/AH-4508-5.html.

22–23　Gladys Carter, quoted in Mary Brooks, "Black WACs Recall Era of Wartime Segregation," *Orlando Sentinel*, September 28, 1992, http://articles.orlandosentinel.com/1992-09-28/news/9209280065_1_women-army-army-auxiliary-corps-women-who-served.

23　Anonymous military letter, quoted in Wayne Drash, "A Midair Courtship: Tuskegee's Historic Love Story," *CNN*, January 23, 2012, https://www.cnn.com/2012/01/22/us/tuskegee-airmen-first-couple/index.html.

24　Kiyo Sato, interview with the author, October 12, 2017.

24　Sato.

25　Sato.

25 Sato.

26 Sato.

28 Mackubin Thomas Owens, "GI Janes, by Stealth," *National Review*, December 9, 2004, https://www .nationalreview.com/2004/12/gi-janes-stealth-mackubin-thomas-owens/.

28 James Gibson, "4 Excuses for Why Women Can't Serve in Combat Debunked," Military1*, February 25, 2015, https://www.military1.com/army/article/565162-4-excuses-for-why-women-cant-serve-in-combat -debunked/.

28 Gibson.

28 Gibson.

28 Gibson.

29 Ash Carter, quoted in Pellerin, "Carter Opens Military Occupations."

29–30 Unnamed male special operative soldiers, quoted in *Considerations for Integrating Women into Closed Occupations in U.S. Special Operations Forces*, Rand, 2016, https://www.rand.org/pubs/research_reports /RR1058.html.

31 Jennifer Smithson (pseudonym), interview with the author, December 19, 2017.

31 Greg Jacob, quoted in Leo Shane III, "Advocates See More Work Ahead for Integrating Women in Combat, Military Roles," *Military Times*, April 5, 2017, https://www.militarytimes.com/news/pentagon -congress/2017/04/05/advocates-see-more-work-ahead-for-integrating-women-in-combat-military -roles/.

31 Male marine sergeant, interview with the author, October 27, 2017.

33 Hanna Bohman, in *Fear Us Women*, produced by Olivia Wilde and Bryn Mooser, 2017, https://www.yahoo .com/lifestyle/olivia-wilde-reveals-brave-lives-isis-fighting-women-new-doc-165458547.html?.tsrc =fauxdal.

34 Smithson, interview.

34–35 Angela Lowe, interview with the author, September 28, 2015.

35 Dharma Klock, interview with the author, November 11, 2017.

35 Shanna Reis, interview with the author, November 6, 2017.

35 Vicky Zorbas Poenitzsch, interview with the author, November 19, 2017.

36 Simone Askew, quoted in Sarah Jorgensen, "First Black Woman to Lead West Point Cadets 'Humbled' by Opportunity," *CNN*, August 15, 2017, http://www.cnn.com/2017/08/15/us/west-point-cadets-simone -askew/index.html.

36 Steven W. Gilland, quoted in Jorgensen, "First Black Woman."

37 Klock, interview.

37 Klock.

37 Smithson, interview.

37 Karen Teague, interview with the author, February 2, 2018.

42 Klock, interview.

42 Kirsten (last name withheld), quoted in Lolita C. Baldor, "Women Get Chance to 'One-Up' the Men in Army Mixed Infantry Units," *Denver Post*, November 26, 2017, http://www.denverpost.com/2017/11/26 /women-army-mixed-infantry-units/.

43 Leigh Ann Hester, quoted in Thom Patterson, "Get Ready for More US Women in Combat," *CNN*, November 11, 2016, http://www.cnn.com/2016/11/10/us/women-combat-us-military/index.html.

44 Kaitlyn Marabello, interview with the author, November 30, 2017.

44 Marabello.

44 "US Army Drill Sergeant," US Army, accessed December 5, 2017, https://www.army.mil/drillsergeant/.

45 Marabello, interview.

45 Marabello.

45 Marabello.

46 Marabello.

46 Marabello.

46 Kelly Kendrick, quoted in Baldor, "Women Get Chance."

46 Kendrick.

46–47 Corbin (last name withheld), quoted in Baldor, "Women Get Chance."

47 Corbin.

47 Andreas Kotsadam, quoted in Alexandra A. Chaidez and A. Daniela Perez, "Reseacher Discusses Gender Integration in Military at Belfer Center," *Harvard Crimson*, October 1, 2017, http://www.thecrimson .com/article/2017/10/2/gender-integration-military-belfer/.

47 Associated Press, "The Marine Corps Is the Only Military Boot Camp That Separates Sexes. That Could Soon Change in Southern California," *LA Times*, August 8, 2017, http://www.latimes.com/nation/nationnow /la-na-women-in-combat-training-20170808-story.html.

48 Austin Renforth, quoted in Hope Hodge Seck, "Marine Boot Camp Now as Integrated as It Should Get, Commander Says," Military.com, June 6, 2017, https://www.military.com/daily-news/2017/06/06 /marine-boot-camp-now-integrated-should-get-commander-says.html.

48 Gillian Thomas, quoted in Shane, "Advocates See More Work."

48 Reginald McClam, quoted in "Female Infantry Marines Will Train, Fight, and Sleep alongside Their Male Counterparts," Task and Purpose, January 26, 2017, https://taskandpurpose.com/field-female-infantry -marines-will-live-train-fight-alongside-male-counterparts/.

48–49 Olumide Onanuga, interview with the author, December 18, 2017.

50 Gregory M. Herek, Oral Statement of Gregory M. Herek, Ph.D, to the House Armed Services Committee, May 5, 1993, https://web.archive.org/web/20160927012407/http://psychology.ucdavis.edu/rainbow/HTML/miltest2.html.

51 Sam Levin, "Top Military Officials Call on Trump to Reverse Transgender Ban," Guardian (US ed.), August 1, 2017, https://www.theguardian.com/us-news/2017/aug/01/donald-trump-transgender-ban-us-military.

52 Mercer, Katie. "Trans Soldier Hits Back at Trump's Army Ban," bTV.com, http://www.barcroft.tv/transgender-military-ban-hayden-brown-donald-trump Accessed July 12, 2018.

53 Scott Miller, in Scott Neuman, "First Female Soldiers Graduate from Army Ranger School," *WBUR/NPR*, August 21, 2015, http://www.wbur.org/npr/433482186/first-female-soldiers-graduate-from-army-ranger-school.

55 Shanna Reis, interview with the author, November 7, 2017.

55–56 Teague, interview.

56 Teague.

56 Teague.

56 Teague, interview, January 30, 2018.

58 Teague, interview, February 2, 2018.

58 Monica Rodriguez, quoted in "Against All Odds: Reunited a Retired Military K-9 with Her First Handler," Rex Specs, accessed March 21, 2018, https://www.rexspecs.com/blogs/news/against-all-odds-reuniting-a-retired-military-k-9-with-her-first-handler.

58 Rodriguez.

59 Brandi Hoeft, quoted in Lauren French, "All-Female Crew Proves Its Chops," *Eau Claire (WI) Leader Telegram*, May 11, 2018, http://www.leadertelegram.com/News/Front-Page/2018/05/11/div-class-libPageBodyLinebreak-All-female-crew-proves-its-chops-div.html.

59 Hoeft.

59 Esperanza Romero, quoted in French, "All-Female Crew."

60 Rodriguez, quoted in Ashley Bunch, "What It's Really Like to Be a Dog Handler in the US Military." *Military Times*, accessed March 21, 2018, https://www.militarytimes.com/2017/06/01/what-it-s-really-like-to-be-a-dog-handler-in-the-us-military/.

60 Rodriguez.

60 Rodriguez, quoted in "Against All Odds."

60 Anna Pongo, interview with the author, November 1, 2017.

60 Pongo.

61 Pongo, interview, December 18, 2017.

61 Pongo.

61 Pongo.

61–62 Pongo.

62 Pongo, interview, November 1, 2017.

62 Ashley Nordmeyer, interview with the author, February 7, 2018.

62 Nordmeyer.

62 Nordmeyer.

63 Nordmeyer.

63 Nordmeyer.

64 Nordmeyer.

64 Cynthia Crate, interview with the author, November 16, 2017.

64 Erica Oliver, interview with the author, October 18, 2017.

64 Vicky Zorbas Poenitzsch, interview with the author, November 19, 2017.

65 Mariah Klenke, quoted in Seck, "Meet the Marine's First Female."

65 Klenke.

66 Ann M. Burkhardt, quoted in Terri Moon Cronk, "DoD Releases Latest Military Sexual Assault Report," Department of Defense, May 1, 2017, https://www.defense.gov/News/Article/Article/1168765/dod -releases-latest-military-sexual-assault-report/.

67 Thomas James Brennan, "Hundreds of Marines Investigated for Sharing Photos of Naked Colleagues," Reveal, March 4, 2017, https://www.revealnews.org/blog/hundreds-of-marines-investigated-for-sharing -photos-of-naked-colleagues/.

68 Christina Cauterucci, quoted in "Marines' Secret Trove of Nonconsensual Nude Photos Is about Power, Not Sex," Slate.com, March 6, 2017, http://www.slate.com/blogs/xx_factor/2017/03/06/the_marines _secret_trove_of_nonconsensual_nude_photos_is_about_power_not.html.

68 Jim Mattis, quoted in Thomas Gibbons-Neff, "How the Marine Corps Widening Nude Photo Scandal Has Spread through the Military," *Washington Post*, March 10, 2017, https://www.washingtonpost.com/news /checkpoint/wp/2017/03/10/how-the-marine-corps-widening-nude-photo-scandal-has-spread -throughout-the-military/?utm_term=.a67402f5264f.

68 Robert B. Neller, quoted in Barbara Starr, "Explicit Photos of Female Marines Posted Online; Navy Investigating," *CNN*, March 6, 2017, http://www.cnn.com/2017/03/05/politics/marines-explicit-photos -investigation/.

69 Erin Kirk Cuomo, quoted in David Martin, "Secret Military Site Posts Explicit Images of Female Service Members," *CBS News*, March 9, 2018, https://www.cbsnews.com/news/hoes-hoin-website-sharing -explicit-photos-of-marines/.

69 Klock, interview, March 27, 2017.

69 Klock.

69–70   Klock.

70   Klock.

70   Crate, interview, November 6, 2017.

70–71   Crate.

71   Crate.

71   Sitaji Gurung, quoted in "Despite Policy Changes, LGBT Military Personnel Still Experiencing Sexual Trauma and Discrimination," City University of New York, press release, January 18, 2018, http://sph.cuny.edu /2018/01/08/lgbt-military-personnel/.

72   "Neglected at Home after Serving Abroad: The Story of Black Women Veterans," African American Policy Forum, June 12, 2018, http://www.aapf.org/black-women-veterans/.

72   Gurung, quoted in "Despite Policy Changes."

73   Don Christensen, quoted in Steff Thomas, "'Me Too' Movement Unmasks Need for Culture Change at DOD," *Federal News Radio*, January 12, 2018, https://federalnewsradio.com/management/2018/01/me -too-movement-unmasks-need-for-culture-change-at-dod/.

74   Juliet Simmons, quoted in Booted: Lack of Recourse for Wrongfully Discharged US Military Rape Survivors, Human Rights Watch, accessed March 21, 2018, https://www.hrw.org/sites/default/files/report_pdf /us0516_militaryweb_1.pdf.

75   "Military Sex Assault Reports Jump 10 Percent in 2017," *PBS*, April 25, 2018, https://www.pbs .org/newshour/nation/military-sex-assault-reports-jump-10-percent-in-2017.

76   Annie Kendzior, quoted in Diana Zoga, "Rape Survivor Calls for Justice Reforms in Military," *NBC Connecticut News*, December 18, 2017, https://www.nbcconnecticut.com/news/national-international /Rape-Survivor-Calls-for-Justice-Reforms-in-Military-464851783.html?_osource=taboola-recirc.

76   Nichole Bowen-Crawford, quoted in Traci Tong, "Women Veterans Want Their Voices Heard in the #MeToo Movement," PRI's the World, January 18, 2018, https://www.pri.org/stories/2018-01-18/women-veterans -want-their-voices-heard-metoo-movement.

76   S.2141—Military Justice Improvement Act of 2017, 115th Congress, Congress.gov, accessed April 21, 2018, https://www.congress.gov/bill/115th-congress/senate-bill/2141.

77–78   Monica Medina, quoted in, "Survivors of Military Sexual Trauma Take the #MeToo Movement to Pentagon's Doors during Demonstration," Service Women's Action Network, January 18, 2018, https://www .servicewomen.org/headlines/10724/.

78   Teague, interview, January 29, 2018.

78   Sexual Assault/Sexual Harassment Response & Prevention, US Army, US Army, accessed February 19, 2018, http://www.sexualassault.army.mil/.

79   Teresa Fazio, quoted in "The Thickest Glass Ceiling in the Marine Corps Breaks," *New York Times*, September 25, 2017, https://www.nytimes.com/2017/09/25/opinion/marine-corps-women-.html ?mcubz=3.

79   Fazio.

80   Kayla Williams, quoted in Lily Casura, "Homeless Women Veterans Struggle to Be Seen," Huffington Post, April 2, 2017, https://www.huffingtonpost.com/entry/homeless-women-veterans-struggle-to-be-seen _us_58e00006e4b0ca889ba1a675.

80   Jenny Pacanowski, quoted in Emily Wax-Thibodeaux, "Female Veterans Say It's Their Time to Write the Memory of War," *Washington Post*, March 30, 2018, https://www.washingtonpost.com/politics/female -veterans-say-its-their-time-to-write-the-memory-of-war/2018/03/30/bc8ea5d4-06a4-11e8-8777 -2a059f168dd2_story.html?utm_term=.f099fa28126b.

81   Disabled American Veterans, quoted in Jerri Bell, "Five Myths about Female Veterans," *Washington Post*, November 10, 2017, https://www.washingtonpost.com/outlook/five-myths/five-myths-about -female-veterans/2017/11/10/31a6398a-c560-11e7-afe9-4f60b5a6c4a0_story.html?utm_term =.a13af3de3452.

81   Allison Jaslow, "VA Has a Woman Problem. It Starts with Its Motto," *Washington Post*, May 29, 2017, https://www.washingtonpost.com/posteverything/wp/2017/05/29/va-motto/?utm_term=.55ca161728d4.

81   "The Origin of the VA Motto Lincoln's Second Inaugural Address," US Department of Veterans Affairs, accessed February 21, 2018, https://www.va.gov/opa/publications/celebrate/vamotto.pdf.

82   Jaslow, quoted in Emily Wax-Thibodeaux, "Is the VA Motto Outdated and Sexist? The Head of the Iraq and Afghanistan Veterans Group Thinks So," *Washington Post*, February 6, 2018, https://www.washingtonpost .com/news/checkpoint/wp/2018/02/06/is-the-va-motto-outdated-and-sexist-the-head-of-the-iraq-and -afghanistan-veterans-group-thinks-so/?utm_term=.e9538d804a39.

82   Williams, letter to Jaslow, *Washington Post*, January 26, 2018, https://www.washingtonpost.com/news /checkpoint/wp-content/uploads/sites/33/2018/02/AJaslowsignedletter.pdf?tid=a_mcntx.

83   Williams.

83   Reis, quoted in Leigh Denoon, "Art Changes Career Path of Veteran," *NPR* interview, accessed March 7, 2018, https://www.wfyi.org/news/articles/veteran-finds-art.

83   Reis.

83–84 Reis.

84   Reis, interview, November 7, 2017.

84   Joana Garcia, interview with the author, March 8, 2018.

84   Sarah Maples, quoted in "The Inconvenience of Being a Woman Veteran," *Atlantic*, November 22, 2017, https://www.theatlantic.com/politics/archive/2017/11/the-inconvenience-of-being-a-woman -veteran/545987/.

84–85 Sidney Goodfriend, quoted in, "New Mentoring Program to Help Women Transition to Civilian Life," US Army Reserve, news release, March 25, 2016, http://www.usar.army.mil/News/Display/Article/704907 /new-mentoring-program-to-help-women-transition-to-civilian-life/.

86   Williams, quoted in Chuck Oldham, "Interview: Kayla M. Williams, Director of the Center for Women Veterans," Defense Media Network, June 20, 2017, https://www.defensemedianetwork.com/stories /interview-kayla-m-williams-director-of-the-center-for-women-veterans/.

86–87 Jay Price, quoted in "Transitioning from Military to Civilian Life Can Be Especially Difficult for Female Veterans," *NPR*, *All Things Considered*, May 30, 2018, https://www.npr.org/2018/05/30/615585074 /transitioning-from-military-to-civilian-life-can-be-especially-difficult-for-fem.

87 Shad Meshad, "Support for Women Veterans: How Long Has This Been Going On?," Huffington Post, August 4, 2017, https://www.huffingtonpost.com/entry/support-for-women-veterans-how-long-has-this -been_us_5984f8ade4b00833d1de2802.

87 BriGette McCoy, quoted in Lily Casura, "GI Jane Needs a Place to Sleep," Huffington Post, April 13, 2017, https://www.huffingtonpost.com/entry/587d14dce4b077a19d181007?timestamp=1485927785845.

87 Jas Boothe, quoted in Casura, "GI Jane."

88 Jas Boothe, quoted in Cortney Willis, "Jas Boothe on Problems Plaguing Female Vets, 'Take a Knee,' and How You Can Help," Grio.com, January 10, 2018, https://thegrio.com/2018/01/10/exclusive-jas-boothe -on-problems-plaguing-female-vets-take-a-knee-and-how-you-can-help/.

90 Smithson, interview, March 28, 2017.

91 Pongo, interview, December 8, 2017.

91 Williams, quoted in Oldham, "Interview."

92 Reis, interview, March 7, 2018.

92 Garcia, interview.

93 Mikie Sherrill, in Anna Brand, "Women Vets Take Aim at a New Target: Public Office," *NBC News*, May 29, 2017, https://www.nbcnews.com/politics/politics-news/women-vets-take-aim-new-target-public -office-n765151.

94 Mary Jennings Hegar, MJ for Texas campaign website, accessed March 24, 2018, http://www.mjfortexas .com/.

94 Chrissy Houlahan, quoted in Brand, "Women Vets."

95 Teague, interview, June 16, 2017.

96 Tammi Jo Shults, quoted in Samantha Schmidt, "Nerves of Steel: She Calmly Landed the Southwest Flight, Just as You'd Expect of a Former Fighter Pilot," *Washington Post*, April 18, 2018, https://www .washingtonpost.com/news/morning-mix/wp/2018/04/18/nerves-of-steel-she-calmly-landed-the -southwest-flight-and-broke-barriers-as-a-fighter-pilot/?noredirect=on&utm_term=.9141529daef3.

96 Shults.

97 Shults.

97 Alfred Tumlinson, quoted in Schmidt, "Nerves."

Glossary

boot camp: the initial training camp for new military recruits. Under strict discipline and rules, recruits learn the history of their military branch and its regulations. Then they go through rigorous physical training and learn to use their rifles or other weapons. A full week is devoted to combat training.

cyber sexual assault: posting nude or graphic photos online without permission of the people in the images. Viewers sometimes post obscene and threatening comments about the people in the photos.

Department of Defense: the branch of the US government charged with coordinating and supervising all agencies and functions of the government involving national security and the US armed forces

deployment: the movement of troops to a place or position for military action. Soldiers may be moved or transferred to a war zone or to a military base in another country.

enlisted service member: a person who joins the military and holds a rank lower than an officer, including ranks such as private, corporal, sergeant, seaman, airman, and gunner.

improvised explosive device (IED): a small, often homemade bomb intended to kill or injure someone. The devices are usually made from easily available materials. Enemy forces may hide them in abandoned buildings, cars, and homes or bury them in roads and ditches.

#MeToo: the Twitter hashtag for the Me Too Movement, in which great numbers of women went public about their experiences of sexual harassment and assault. The movement took off in October 2017 after dozens of female celebrities came forward to accuse prominent men of sexual harassment and assault.

military occupational specialty: a job—such as military police or special electronic devices repair—available in branches of the military. Specific job codes describe each type of job. For example, 31B is for military police, and 94F is for special electronic devices repairer.

military sexual trauma: repeated instances of being sexually harassed, sexually assaulted, or both during military service

military working dog: a dog, often a Belgian Malinois or German shepherd, trained by the military to detect drugs or improvised explosive devices and to patrol and guard bases and other military facilities

National Guard: one of the reserve components of the military, run by individual states. Members of the National Guard serve a specified number of days each year. They usually hold civilian jobs, and the US government calls them to active duty when required. The National Guard often assists in state emergencies and natural disasters.

officer: a military member who has authority over enlisted members. To be an officer requires more education and training than for enlistees. Officer ranks include lieutenant, captain, major, colonel, admiral, and general.

Pentagon: headquarters of the Department of Defense near Washington, DC, in Arlington County, Virginia. The Pentagon is the world's largest office building.

post-traumatic stress disorder (PTSD): a mental health condition triggered by traumatic events such as battle, serious injury, or seeing others die. The condition may cause nightmares, depression, anxiety, and terrifying flashbacks.

Purple Heart: a military decoration given to service members (or their families) who are wounded or killed in action

Reserve Officers' Training Corps (ROTC): a college program in which students take military courses in leadership and courses required for their degree. Graduates become military officers and quickly move into leadership positions.

reserves: a component of the US military similar to the National Guard. Unlike the National Guard, the US government runs the reserves rather than individual US states. Reserves serve a specified number of days a year and may be called to active duty.

sexual assault: sexual contact that usually involves force without consent or with a person incapable of giving consent or with a person who considers the assailant to hold a position of trust or authority over the victim

sexual harassment: repeated instances of unwelcome sexual advances, requests for sexual favors, sexual innuendoes, and obscene comments

Sexual Harassment/Assault Response and Prevention (SHARP): a program designed to control, reduce, and eliminate sexual harassment and assault among military staff. Each branch of the US military provides this mandatory training to all personnel.

special forces: elite forces within the US military that specialize in covert (secret) missions. Special force members receive extensive training. The forces include the Army Rangers, Navy SEALs (Sea, Air, and Land forces), and Green Berets, among others.

veteran: a person who served in the military, whether at war or in peace, in the US or foreign countries

Veterans Administration (VA): the federal agency that oversees and provides services for veterans. Services include health care (clinics and hospitals), housing, job training, and education.

Selected Bibliography

Associated Press. "The Marine Corps Is the Only Military Boot Camp That Separates Sexes. That Could Soon Change in Southern California." *Los Angeles Times*, August 8, 2017. http://www.latimes.com/nation/nationnow/la-na-women-in-combat-training-20170808 -story.html.

Bell, Jerri. "Five Myths about Female Veterans." *Washington Post*, November 10, 2017. https://www.washingtonpost.com/outlook/five-myths/five-myths-about-female -veterans/2017/11/10/31a6398a-c560-11e7-afe9-4f60b5a6c4a0_story.html?utm _term=.a13af3de3452.

Brand, Anna. "Women Vets Take Aim at a New Target: Public Office." *NBC News*, May 29, 2017. https://www.nbcnews.com/politics/politics-news/women-vets-take-aim-new-target-public -office-n765151.

Brennan, Thomas James. "Hundreds of Marines Investigated for Sharing Photos of Naked Colleagues." Reveal, March 4, 2017. https://www.revealnews.org/blog/hundreds-of -marines-investigated-for-sharing-photos-of-naked-colleagues/.

Casura, Lily. "Into the Gap: Women Veterans Describe Homelessness." *Huffington Post*, September 16, 2017. https://www.huffingtonpost.com/entry/5898228ce4b02bbb1816bc76 ?timestamp=1486452140644.

Cronk, Terri Moon. "DOD Releases Latest Military Sexual Assault Report." Department of Defense, May 1, 2017. https://www.defense.gov/News/Article/Article/1168765/dod-releases-latest -military-sexual-assault-report/.

Fazio, Teresa. "The Thickest Glass Ceiling in the Marine Corps Breaks." *New York Times*, September 25, 2017. https://www.nytimes.com/2017/09/25/opinion/marine-corps -women-.html?mcubz=3.

Hegar, Mary Jennings. *Shoot like a Girl: One Woman's Dramatic Fight in Afghanistan and on the Home Front*. New York: Penguin, 2017.

Maples, Sarah. "The Inconvenience of Being a Woman Veteran." *Atlantic*, November 22, 2017. https://www.theatlantic.com/politics/archive/2017/11/the-inconvenience-of-being-a -woman-veteran/545987/.

Oldham, Chuck. "Interview: Kayla M. Williams, Director of the Center for Women Veterans." Defense Media Network, June 20, 2017. https://www.defensemedianetwork.com/stories /interview-kayla-m-williams-director-of-the-center-for-women-veterans/.

Shane, Leo, III. "Advocates See More Work Ahead for Integrating Women in Combat, Military Roles." *Military Times*, April 5, 2017. https://www.militarytimes.com/news/pentagon -congress/2017/04/05/advocates-see-more-work-ahead-for-integrating-women-in -combat-military-roles/.

Wakeman, Sarah Rosetta. *An Uncommon Soldier: The Civil War Letters of Sarah Rosetta Wakeman, Alias Private Lyons Wakeman, 153rd Regiment, New York State Volunteers*. Edited by Lauren Cook Burgess. Pasadena, MD: Minerva Center, 1994.

Further Information

BOOKS

Biank, Tanya. *Undaunted: the Real Story of America's Servicewomen in Today's Military.* New York: New American Library, 2013. Follow the military lives of four women: a marine drill instructor, a marine general, an army platoon leader, and an army major over the course of several years. Learn about their challenges, successes, and the military's impact on their personal lives as they make their way through the male-dominated military.

Blanton, Deanne, and Lauren M. Cook. *They Fought like Demons: Women Soldiers in the Civil War.* New York: Vintage Books, 2001. Read about a few of the several hundred women who dressed as men and fought in the American Civil War. The book explores their reasons for joining and the women's wartime experiences.

Buckley, Gail Lumet. *American Patriots: The Story of Blacks in the Military from the Revolution to Desert Storm.* New York: Random House, 2002. This fascinating book chronicles stories of African American women and men who served in the military, even while facing racism and desegregation at home and in the service. Through interviews, photos, and other research, the author introduces us to some of the brave service members whose courage and determination changed the course of American history.

Gershick, Zsa. *Secret Service: Untold Stories of Lesbians in the Military.* Los Angeles: Alyson Books, 2005. Published prior to the repeal of the Don't Tell, Don't Ask rule, the book says 79 percent of Americans supported allowing gay and lesbian troops to serve openly at the time. The author blasts the assertion that those service members who served openly would break down morale and unit cohesion. Women profiled in the book tell of their military experiences, often marked by harassment, fear, and dishonorable discharges.

Goldsmith, Connie. *Dogs at War: Military Canine Heroes.* Minneapolis: Twenty-First Century Books, 2017. Through numerous personal interviews, see how the US military selects and trains military working dogs and their handlers, and the jobs they perform during war and in peace in every branch of the US military. Their handlers adopt many of these dogs at retirement, and they live the rest of their lives as happy family dogs.

Higgins, Nadia Abushanab. *Feminism: Reinventing the F-Word.* Minneapolis: Twenty-First Century Books, 2016. Explore the history of feminism through pioneers such as Elizabeth Cady Stanton, Betty Friedan, Shirley Chisholm, Gloria Steinem, and more. Meet twenty-first-century leaders who are striving to empower women at work, in government, and at home. The right to serve in the military was a goal of the early feminist movement.

Holmstedt, Kirsten. *Band of Sisters: American Women at War in Iraq*: Mechanicsburg, PA: Stackpole Books, 2007. This award-winning book follows four female American soldiers during their tour in Iraq, including the first American female pilot to be shot down and survive, the first black female pilot in combat, a turret gunner defending convoys, and a nurse working to save lives. While this book was published before woman could serve in combat, it shows that women were actually serving in combat long before the official ruling in 2015. The book includes a foreword by Iraq War veteran and US senator Tammy Duckworth.

Jones, Patrick. Support and Defend series. Minneapolis: Darby Creek, 2015. This series of four short novels focuses on teens from diverse backgrounds and highlights many of the challenges that US military families face. The deployment of one or both of their parents affected about two million or more children and teens. Teens may experience anxiety, stress, fear, and may have problems with sleep and schoolwork.

Lemmon, Gayle Tzemach. *Ashley's War*. New York: HarperCollins, 2015. In 2010 the US Army created a secret program to insert women into special operations units in Afghanistan. Women accompanied men on raids, questioning females living at suspected enemy compounds. Afghanistan is a Muslim nation, and Islamic law prohibits men from questioning or searching women, so female soldiers gathered crucial information that male soldiers could not have obtained.

Mundy, Liza. *Code Girls: The Untold Story of the American Women Code Breakers of World War II*. New York: Hachette Books, 2017. American women could not serve in combat during World War II. They served in many other ways. For example, the US Navy and the US Army recruited ten thousand women and taught them how to break codes. Their work translating important military messages from enemy nations shortened the war, saved countless lives, and gave women access to careers previously denied to them.

WEBSITES

The American Military Partner Association
https://militarypartners.org/
This nonprofit organization is the nation's largest organization of lesbian, gay, bisexual, transgender, and queer (LGBTQ) military families and their allies. It has fifty thousand members and supporters. The mission is to connect, support, honor, and serve the partners, spouses, families, and allies of LGBTQ service members.

Center for Women Veterans
https://www.va.gov/womenvet/
Specifically developed for women veterans, the site offers extensive information about health care, education, pensions, home loans, and other veteran benefits. It includes sections for the veteran and her family, as well as employment and training resources.

Final Salute
http://www.finalsaluteinc.org/
The mission of Final Salute is to provide homeless women veterans with safe housing. The organization estimates that the United States has fifty-five thousand homeless women veterans on any given day. The organization has provided more than 12,600 days of transitional housing for homeless women and their children since 2011. The organization also assists with food, clothing, childcare, and other support for homeless women veterans and their children.

Iraq and Afghanistan Veterans of America
https://iava.org/
The organization's mission is to connect, unite, and empower post-9/11 veterans. It has more than four hundred thousand members. It was founded by and led by veterans. The advocacy group supports veterans in their transition to civilian life.

Military OneSource
https://www.militaryonesource.mil/
Military OneSource is a confidential Department of Defense-funded program providing comprehensive information on every aspect of military life at no cost to active duty, National Guard, and reserve members and their families. The organization provides information related to deployment, reunion, relationships, grief, spouse employment and education, parenting, and childhood services.

National Association for Black Vets
http://nabvets.org/
This veterans group advocates for its members with the federal government as well as with administrators in states, counties, and cities. The organization assists veterans seeking claims against the US Department of Veterans Affairs. It strives to create positive lifestyles for veterans and their families and is working to preserve the historical record for minority veterans.

National Veterans Foundation
https://nvf.org/contact/
This site provides vet-to-vet phone or email communication, with information about benefits, jobs, and news. The site has a women's section and includes a Lifeline for Vets call-in number at 888-777-4443 for immediate help.

Service Women's Action Network
https://www.servicewomen.org/
https://www.facebook.com/servicewomen/
The group's mission is to support, connect, and advocate for servicewomen. The related Facebook site offers events, photos, videos, jobs, and many posts about the group's activities.

Veterans Crisis Line
https://www.veteranscrisisline.net/
Veterans in crisis and their loved ones can reach a live person 24/7 for confidential assistance at 800-273-8255. They can text or enter an online chat. Many staff members at the crisis line are veterans, and all are trained to work with veteran-related issues. The line has taken thirty-three million calls since 2007 and tens of thousands of texts and online chats.

Women in the Military
https://www.military.com/topics/women-military
This site contains numerous articles about women actively serving in the military as well as information about the roles they fill, success stories, and other news of special interest to women service members. Other sections have information for military families and military life in general and a broad selection of informative videos.

AUDIO, MOVIES, AND VIDEOS

Army Basic Training. New York: Originals/Lou Reda Productions. Military.com video, 4:39. Posted July 15, 2015. http://www.military.com/video/forces/army-training/original-army -basic-training/4355828494001. Watch women and men navigate the ten-week boot camp, from arrival on army buses and getting uniforms, to weapons training and graduation day.

"*Fear Us Women* Trailer." YouTube video, 2:13. Posted by Ryot, November 8, 2017. https://www.youtube.com/watch?v=mpMDnx9Ux6g. This is a trailer of the film *Fear Us Women*, directed by David Darg. You will meet Hanna Bohman and others who serve in the Women's Protection Unit in Syria. Known in Kurdish as the YPJ, the unit is an all-female military organization that includes Kurds, Arabs, Assyrians, and foreign fighters in Syria. The unit numbers about twenty-four thousand women who fight the terrorist organization ISIS in Syria and work to bring women's rights to the region.

"Honor. Purpose. Challenge: Women of the Seabees and Civil Engineer Corps." YouTube video, 5:46. Posted by Navy Facilities Engineering Command, October 11, 2011. https://www .youtube.com/watch?v=T_2Fry-QbgI&feature=youtu.be. Navy Seabees (construction workers) and engineers work around the world providing humanitarian help in disasters. They also perform construction work on US military bases. In this video, female Seabees talk about the value of their work.

"A Purple Heart Warrior Takes Aim at Military Inequality in '*Shoot like a Girl*'" 43:01. *National Public Radio, Fresh Air*, March 2, 2017. https://www.npr.org/programs/fresh-air/2017 /03/02/518135948/fresh-air-for-march-2-2017. Host Terry Gross interviews Mary Jennings Hegar, author of *Shoot Like a Girl*. Before the military allowed women in combat roles, Hegar copiloted a medevac helicopter in Afghanistan that the Taliban shot down. Although wounded, she returned fire, saving the lives of her crew and onboard patients.

"US Marines Get First Female Infantry Officer." *BBC* video, 0:50. http://www.bbc.com/news /world-us-canada-41394646. In this brief film clip, watch the first female marine infantry officer with her team as they train in an undisclosed mountainous desert environment.

"USS *Theodore Roosevelt* Night Flight Operations." YouTube video, 2:31. Posted by the US Navy, July 8, 2015. https://www.youtube.com/watch?v=GEJJx4v-6-s. Watch as jet pilots land and take off from the *USS Roosevelt* aircraft carrier. An all-female crew performed this complex and strenuous work to demonstrate they are as capable as men are.

"Women in Combat, in Their Own Words. *Atlantic* video, 4:36, January 11, 2016. https://www .theatlantic.com/video/index/423600/women-in-combat/. In this short video, hear from US military women trained as cultural support teams to support special operations units gathering information from local communities in Iraq and Afghanistan.

Index

Photo Acknowledgments

Image credits: Scott Olson/Getty Images, p. 1; Bob Daemmrich/Alamy Stock Photo, p. 5; © American Antiquarian Society/Bridgeman Images, p. 10; U.S. Army photo by Spc. Jeremy D. Crisp, p. 11; The Granger Collection, New York, p. 13; Bettmann/Getty Images, p. 16; Library of Congress (LC-DIG-npcc-09951), pp. 17, 22; Everette Collection Inc/Alamy Stock Photo, p. 19; U.S. Air Force, p. 20; Library of Congress, p. 22; Gado Images/Alamy Stock Photo, p. 23; Courtesy Lisa Kato, p. 25; Efrain Padro/Alamy Stock Photo, p. 27; David Turnley/Corbis/VCG/Getty Images, p. 29; DANIEL MIHAILESCU/AFP/Getty Images, p. 32; Deniz/Barcroft Images/Barcroft Media/Getty Images, p. 33; Courtesy of the Author, p. 35; AP Photo/Austin Lachance/U.S. Army, p. 36; Laura Westlund/Independent Picture Service, pp. 40, 72–73; Scott Olson/Getty Images, pp. 43, 49; U.S. Air Force, p. 50; Barcroft Images/Barcroft Mediay/Getty Images, p. 52; Jessica McGowan/Getty Images, p. 53; © U.S. Army, p. 61; U.S. Navy photo by Matthew Konopka, p. 63; Lance Cpl Anabel Abreu Rodriguez/U.S. Marines, p. 65; Leigh Vogel/Getty Images, p. 67; Chip Somodevilla/Getty Images, pp. 75, 89; AP Photo/Scott Applewhite, p. 77; © U.S. Army Graphic, p. 78; Steve Mack/Getty Images, p. 81; U.S. Army, p. 85; Chris Maddaloni/CQ Roll Call/Getty Images, p. 88; Austin Teague Photography, p. 92; Maddie McGarvey/The New York Times, p. 94; Andrew Harrer-Pool/Getty Images, p. 96.

Front Cover: DanielBendjy/E+/Getty Images.

Back Cover: VZ1/Shutterstock.com.